JACQUELINE GETCHIUS, MA, LPCC

That's My Mom

Healing from Emotional Neglect

This book was professionally typeset on Reedsy.
Find out more at reedsy.com

To my everlasting love, Tom.
To my boy, my joy, Gavin.
To the WOWZAs, friends who are family.

"We are the unwitting carriers of our parents' secrets, the ripples made by stones we never saw thrown."

—Erica Bauermeister.

Contents

1

Introduction

"Don't lose your nerve," I warned myself as I eased up the narrow, wooden stairs to the private gathering space at the coffee shop that I had reserved days prior. Planning being my spiritual gift is a joke my husband likes to rib me on. But the reality was, like many of my life's moments, I had thought out this moment meticulously ahead of time to try to make it go as smoothly as possible. Finding whatever I could control equaled a slight alleviation of my anxiety about the unknown. Only a brief minute after I settled at a table in the quiet room, my dad walked in.

With only a smattering of gray, his thick, straight, dark brown hair and slim stature gave him the appearance of being younger than his sixty-six years. His yellowed teeth from thirty years of smoking, though, made him appear more weathered. Dressed in his typical dad attire of faded jeans, a sweatshirt from his pride and joy alma mater, Purdue, and generic tennis shoes, he was quiet but said, "Hello," and took a seat at the table. I immediately dived in by thanking him for meeting me and cut to the chase reading aloud a letter that I had written to him.

In my letter, I delicately outlined the concerns regarding my relationship, if you could call it that, with my mother. Through plump tears that silently washed down my face, I detailed how my mental health had suffered and how I had experienced periods of having suicidal thoughts in the past because of how emotionally neglectful my mother was. Through shallow, shaky breaths,

I verbalized how I yearned to try to find a way to coexist with my mother in a way that no longer affected me negatively. As I progressed through my letter, I grew more assertive, but still proceeded cautiously in sharing the details of the boundaries I wanted my mom to respect. I had tried briefly, and admittedly quite timidly, to glance up at my dad while I was reading the letter. But his face was awash with anger, the muscles in his jaw clenched and pulsating, so I quickly decided it was not helpful to make eye contact, and instead read the remainder of the letter without looking up any further.

When I finished reading through the words of my letter, my dad appeared furious and slowly shook his head from side to side. The first words out of his mouth were, "That's not my wife."

I boldly and without a second thought responded by saying, "Well, that's my mom."

"That's my mom," would become a pivotal phrase to me. With the help of my therapist, it would be heralded as a simple, concise way of speaking my truth.

Despite being a psychotherapist myself for nearly ten years at this point, I still relied upon the guidance and wisdom of my own therapist to open my eyes to the often subtle, but all too real damage my mother had had on my emotional wellbeing and my sense of self.

———————-

Fast forward to six years later and I find myself back in a coffee shop in the 'burbs of Minneapolis, iced coconut milk latte in hand, but this time drafting the very book you're reading. I have now been a psychotherapist for 15 years and own a private practice, Wellspring Women's Counseling, where I work with women who have found themselves in a similar place in life that I was not long ago. It was a smoldering, slow-burning dream that gained more and more momentum, to put words to the experience I had with my mother in book form.

This book details my journey of discovering and naming my experience of emotional neglect, setting boundaries to prevent further pain, and finding peace by trusting my gut and following a path in my life that was right for me. I took the leap to no longer allow the status quo of emotional neglect to invade every facet of my life. Today as I'm pushing up against my 40th year of life, I can affirm that I have more self-confidence and serenity in my life than I ever have before. Don't get me wrong, there are still plenty of daily stressors and disappointments that I face, but I now have an innate shield of self-protection that allows me to trust my own strengths and skills to better weather storms as they come my way.

My aspiration and purpose of this book is to shine a light on the rarely discussed, but incredibly real experience of emotional neglect. Emotional neglect can feel like an invisible and shameful experience. It is a form of emotional abuse. Abuse of any kind is a form of trauma and can have long-lasting deep-seated effects on our bodies, our memories, and our sense of self. My aim is to give you the words to label your experience, understand the nuances of it, and how to heal and find a path past it.

I intend to shine a light on the subtle, yet impactful ways that emotional neglect shows up in our relationships, especially with our primary caregivers. For me, emotional neglect came from my mom. Once emotional neglect is better recognized, there is often a light bulb moment where you may find yourself saying, "That's exactly what I experienced!" The emotional neglect club is not one that brings pride in belonging to it, but you don't have to stay a member of this club forever. Instead, as I will outline for you as your read on, you have options. You do not have to stay immersed in this painful place forever. But because of the very fact that emotional neglect is unnoticed by the naked eye and often not readily recognized, it can take many years to finally confront it. This is what I experienced myself. I found that by writing my own life story and outlining the ways that emotional neglect played out in my life and impacted my sense of self, self-confidence, and contentment in life, I was able to derive strength through my lived experience. I am a survivor. You are too.

This book is a helping hand I've put into the world just for you. You may feel alone or afraid to acknowledge what you have experienced. I've been there too. As I will show you, though, this doesn't have to be the way you feel forever. I eventually gained the courage to confront my own mother's emotional neglect and assert what I truly needed to feel, valued as a person and cared for like a daughter. You too will find renewed confidence in what you deserve to feel in key relationships in your life. I will give you strategies for self-preservation as you work through your painful lived experience. I will shine a light on how to find the right kind of support to help you confront this traumatic relationship dynamic in your life. Finally, I will share what different choices you have when you feel ready to move forward in your healing journey. Take my hand and let's dive in. We've got this.

2

Days of My Life

Most trauma returns to us in flashbacks. Quick, brief, snippets of time. These memories are ingrained in our emotional memory that can either slowly reveal themselves to us or more suddenly pop into our awareness when we are ready to grasp their meaning.

One of the earliest specks of memories where it started to resonate that the relationship with my mother was atypical and not the kind of relationship I longed for, was after a simple trip to a thrift store. I was eight years old with my trademark pigtails to contain my wild brownish-red curls. Slowly I meandered through the aisles and eventually picked out a simple framed photo displaying the silhouette of a mother and daughter holding hands while walking down a dirt path. I used my own carefully saved allowance money to pay for this trinket. Across the photo, the text was scrawled saying, "My Mother, My Friend," with a touching poem about how mothers are always there for support and love.

My Mother, my friend so dear
  Throughout my life, you're always near
  A tender smile to guide my way
  You're the sunshine to light my day

As I hung this framed photo up on my pastel pink bedroom wall, I gazed through my green eyes at it reflectively. I spent a lot of time lost in deep reflection as a child, often in my small bedroom, quietly curled up reading or playing with my dolls as my mother couldn't be bothered to play with me. I would pile all my stuffed animals onto my bed and immerse myself in a cocoon of improvised comfort as my own self-soothing practice. During this specific moment of reflection, I felt a lump swell up in my throat telling me that the words on this frame were a lie. My mother wasn't my friend. My mother wasn't supportive or loving. But I so deeply wanted to believe this photo and the words across it as truth. I kept the photo on my wall for years, maybe as a hope or omen that the poem could become true. Instead, it was a constant reminder of the knotting tension I felt between what I wanted the relationship with my mother to be, and what it actually was.

Being a reflective thinker can be a gift and a curse. Later in adulthood when my therapist, Delia, introduced me to a book called "The Highly Sensitive Person" by Elaine Aron, you could say I found "my people" by identifying with this label. Highly sensitive persons feel things more deeply than their peers and yearn to process things on a more profound level. This book gave me insight into why my mind works the way it does. Previously I thought that I simply over-analyzed everything. But the words in this book revealed that others shared in this way of taking in the world on a deeper level and it was profoundly reinforcing to my fragile ego.

Because I was frequently lost in reflection, I have often been mislabeled as an introvert. But the reality is that I identify more as an extrovert. Extroverts crave being around others as this is where they get their energy. I don't actually thrive with alone time and tend to be more motivated and activated when I have a circle of others around me. I feel joy in togetherness. Left alone, I often feel depleted.

I may have been born more extroverted by nature, but with my mother's hands-off approach to parenting, I was often left swimming in a world that left me overwhelmed and alone. This solitary overthinking began a downward spiral gaining momentum leading to excessive worry which led to restlessness which then led to anxiety.

Being self-identified as deeply reflective, I spent a great amount of time pondering the relationships in my life. I have always been someone who values relationships above all. Because of this, I recognized early on that I had a profound need to feel connected to others. I realized that I wanted to feel close bonds with others, where we could be there for each other, have in-depth meaningful conversations, and trust that our relationship was a priority.

Even as a child, I not only valued relationships, but I was constantly analyzing them and soaking up information about relationship dynamics like a sponge. I paid attention to facial expressions and what often went unsaid in interactions between people. This is probably why as an adult I was so drawn to studying the field of Psychology.

How birth order impacts relationship dynamics was an area of Psychology that particularly piqued my attention. I was the oldest child in my family with one brother who was four years my junior. My dad was the youngest of three siblings in his family, and my mom was the middle child of nine siblings. Yes, that's right, NINE. Where one falls in birth order in their family can have a very real impact on their personality.

Researchers Flowers and Brown found that firstborns, due to their perceived responsibility to perform leadership duties, tend to become more anxious in stressful situations than younger siblings. Interestingly, the youngest children in a family experience enhanced investment from their parents as they represent the last opportunity for parents to invest in their offspring. Furthermore, the youngest kids in the family are less likely to be perfectionists and have an increased tendency to need more pampering or caretaking. The youngest child in a family is even noted to tend to seek to achieve goals through passive or manipulative means, such as using charm, persuasion, complaints, or guilt, and often try to please others to gain significance within the family system.

Even at my friends' houses, I watched in fascination the encounters between family members. This is likely what began to increase an awareness inside me early on that my family, but more specifically, that my mother, was different from my friends' mothers. Because I recognized an eccentricity in my mother, I realized my family system was wholly different than my friends' families in many subtle but important ways.

For instance, in my modest-sized home growing up, there was a TV in nearly every room of the house, including the kitchen and dining room. In fact, the only rooms that didn't have TVs were the bathroom and laundry room. For every single meal we ate at home, my family would sit together at the dinner table with the TV on. The TV was like the fifth family member beside me, my parents, and my younger brother. It was ever-present, no matter what. When I was in fourth grade, I asked if we could turn the TV off for dinner one night so we could talk and chat as a family. You know, talk, connect, something meaningful.

My mother responded with a flat, "No, we like having it on."

Of course, my request really had nothing to do with the TV. I was instead asking in my own child-sized way for connection. I wanted my mother's attention. For quality time together as a family. What I read between these words was that my mom valued silently absorbing whatever show was on the TV more than she valued forging a relationship with her daughter or family. It didn't matter that I yearned for quality time together without distraction. This is just what we did every night and there was no chance of changing that. I remember sitting somewhat dumbfounded when I would have dinner at a friend's house, that their family sat down together at a table without a TV blaring in the background. Instead, my friends' families communally talked about their days during dinner. They laughed and enjoyed each other's company. I didn't have a single friend who actually had a TV in their dining room like my family.

TV time during dinner almost always included watching the evening news, thus, hearing a daily flood of stories about murder, robbery, rape, and a host of other horrific topics not appropriate for a young child. Hearing these alarming accounts of crime night after night brewed growing anxiety in my small body. When what you are bombarded with day after day focuses on the worst-case scenarios in life, you begin to form your own interpretation of the world based on this.

So, as the young little girl sitting at the dining room table, I began to see that these crimes and atrocities were a likely and inevitable part of life.

Dr. Bessel Van Der Kolk, MD poignantly defined trauma in his book, *The Body Keeps the Score*, as "anything that overwhelms our system." This wide definition makes sense of the many subtle ways a person can end up feeling traumatized. For me, my own little kid system was repeatedly, day after day, being overwhelmed by the fear that something like what I was watching on TV could and would happen to me and my family.

When our bodies experience a trauma, it affects the baseline that our nervous system rests at. The anxiety and fear that trauma brings make it so that our nervous system is always armed and ready for any threat that could mean it needs to fight or flee from. When you are always in this state of hyper-arousal, it's exhausting to your body. It means anything else that startles your system can easily throw your body into a completely overwhelmed state. My parents didn't seem to understand or see the connection that all this exposure to traumatic news stories was having on my recurrent nightmares, fear of being separated from my family, anxiety about trying new things, or really anything that could result in injury. This explains why it took me a great many years before I worked up the courage to learn how to ride a bike without training wheels because of all the danger and risks it brought to my eyes. Or why going to school frequently left me in tears because I didn't know what was going to happen to my family while I was away.

Because my mom didn't consistently have a job out of the home until I was almost out of elementary school, summers and breaks from school always included, you guessed it, loads of TV time. My mom sat on our red velvet couch and watched all the major soap operas on TV. I've seen Stefano killed off *Days of Our Lives* more times than I can count. I joined in to at least be in close physical proximity to my mom. Since my mom was glued to the TV, I figured, why not at least try to spend time with her this way by joining her on the couch. I remember around the age of seven asking my mom while we were watching *Days of Our Lives* what the word "rape" meant, which I had heard referred to countless times on the soap operas.

She responded in her typical way, without feeling or elaboration, "To force someone to have sex with you."

I didn't know what sex was and I didn't ask for further explanation. There was always an unspoken rule that my mom wasn't interested in any sort of in-depth conversations with me. It was best to keep quiet and keep my thoughts to myself. Instead, we just continued to use TV to pass the time away. My favorite movies as a young child (we're talking ages six through ten) were *Dirty Dancing* and *Pretty Woman*. Often, I sat and watched TV alone. What else was there to do? My mom had no interest in playing with me. At least when I watched TV, I could see others interacting even though I had no one to play with myself. Again, it didn't occur to me until later in adulthood how the sexual themes of my favorite movies were far from appropriate for a child. Additionally, there was never a limit put on TV time in my house. There was no encouragement for me to play or my mom inviting me to play with her. In many ways, it seemed like TV was the buffer in my family, the babysitter, and certainly more highly valued than the children in our family.

TV brought boundary issues that I couldn't recognize or articulate as a child but realized later as an adult that made my stomach turn in an uncomfortable way. Boundaries are essential in healthy relationships. They provide rules or limits created to make a person feel safe in a relationship. Without proper boundaries, a person is left feeling depleted, taken advantage of, taken for granted, or intruded upon which can lead to resentment, hurt, and anger.

Absorbing interactions at my friends' houses was also how I came to realize another stark difference between their families compared to mine. My friends' mothers gave their children affection. I witnessed this loving affection taking the forms of hugs, kisses, cuddles, and caring pats on the back. How deeply my heart hurt when I saw my friend's mothers show their love for their children through these acts of affection! At my home, affection was almost nonexistent. The only exception was that my mother would give me a rote, stiff, routine kiss on the head each night when I went to bed, but that was where affection started and ended. This act from my mom did not feel loving, but instead felt obligatory and like something to be checked off a to-do list. I remember feeling genuine shock when a friend's mother gave me a loving hug when I was saying goodbye after a play date. It was such an unusual thing to me that I was taken aback. Not in a bad way, but in a surprising way.

As an adult, I later realized how much I needed physical affection to feel loved. It's sad to admit, but I didn't realize this until I had friends and later a husband who gave me the hugs that I had never realized I so desperately needed. I felt transformed by hugs. It was as if I was getting a bucket filled that had long been dried up.

As a child, I would go so far as to go out on a limb and ask timidly my mom, "Can I have a hug?"

She would occasionally comply, but only after a sarcastic, exasperated sigh. Then the hug itself was stiff, cold, brief, and forced. There was no warmth there. Her begrudging hugs made me feel worse rather than better. It felt like I was burdening her by asking for this simple act. I began to feel like there was something wrong with me that my own mother didn't want to hug me. It wasn't too far a leap to wonder, maybe she just didn't love me?

To form a healthy attachment with their child, a parent needs to show them positive regard in an unconditional fashion. Assor, Roth, and Deci found in their 2004 study of the emotional costs of parents' conditional regard, that when this happens, it nurtures a child's growth not just physically but psychologically. In contrast, conditional regard or consistent disregard instead leads to a child having a conditional sense of self-worth and feelings of shame following failure.

Additionally, Winston and Chicot found in their 2016 study on the importance of early bonding on the long-term mental health and resilience of children, that building a strong emotional connection with someone takes paying attention to the other person, trust, emotional availability, showing affection, fighting fair, and seeing the world through their eyes. By doing these things, you build a bond with another person. There is increasing evidence from the fields of developmental psychology, neurobiology, and animal epigenetic studies showing that neglect, parental inconsistency, and lack of love can lead to long-term mental health problems, reduced overall potential, and happiness.

There were countless moments that reinforced this internalized feeling that my mother didn't care about me or love me. My mom didn't like to play with me. Once in a great while, she would play a board game with my brother and me, but for the most part, we were on our own.

Unlike my mom, my dad would play with my brother. My brother was the energizer bunny as a child. He was four years younger than me, very slim, and always on the go. My brother and dad were both into sports, being outside and active playing baseball, basketball, and riding bikes. This really wasn't my cup of tea as a kid. You could say I was "indoorsy." I was much more content to color, make friendship bracelets, and play with Barbies. My brother didn't enjoy these activities and since my mom couldn't be bothered to engage in these activities with me, I was left to my own devices to play by myself. Narrative therapy theory posits that as we experience different interactions and events, we give meaning to those experiences and they subsequently influence how we view ourselves and our world. The more I saw and experienced all of these moments in my life, it reinforced my internalized feeling that my mother didn't care about me.

When I was in elementary school, we lived in a small Victorian-era home nearly a hundred years old. It was three stories tall with frighteningly steep stairs leading up to the finished attic space we used as a playroom. The only window on the third story was a tiny circle about a foot in diameter. I could frequently be found daydreaming out of this window, often feeling like Rapunzel staring down at the street below and feeling utterly alone.

It wasn't just having to play by myself that created a deep hurt in my soul. In third grade, while studying for a spelling bee and trying to cram in as many words in my brain as possible, I became overwhelmed and started sobbing. If I was distraught and crying for any number of common childhood reasons, my mother did not give me physical comfort or affection. She never said kind, caring words to help me calm down. Instead, I would most often go to my pink-covered room, lie on my pink bedspread, and cry until there were no more tears left. If my dad were home, he would reliably come up the stairs to my room and give me a hug or rub my back and talk to me about my feelings as best he was able. My dad was the one parent who seemed to recognize that his daughter needed that physical and emotional comfort. The problem was that my dad was a workaholic and for much of my childhood, had a round trip commute of three hours a day to work and back, so he just wasn't home enough to be there physically or emotionally for me.

Years later when I was studying Psychology at Luther College, I became enlightened regarding the different kinds of attachment styles that children have to their mothers. Attachment theory was developed dating back to the 1960s by John Bowlby and Mary Ainsworth. Their theory was based on the understanding that mothers who are present and responsive to their child's needs create a safe base from which their child can venture forth with confidence to explore the world and return for comfort. Research has identified four types of attachment including secure attachment, anxious-insecure attachment, avoidant-insecure attachment, and disorganized-insecure attachment. The preferred outcome is a secure attachment which occurs when mothers are available, sensitive, responsive and accepting of their child. These parents pick their children up, play with them, and reassure them, teaching them someone will help them process their emotions. Alternatively, when a parent minimizes their child's feelings, rejects their demands, and doesn't help them with difficulties, it can lead to an avoidant-insecure attachment.

What I gleaned was that due to my mother's lack of responsiveness, I had developed an avoidant-insecure attachment to her. What does this mean? Children who have this type of attachment style learn not to seek out their mother when distressed. Kids learn that their mom is insensitive, rejecting, and unavailable during times of emotional sorrow. It was with a wave of sadness as an adult, thinking of myself as a young girl realizing that when she needed comfort, she was ultimately on her own to comfort herself.

And boy did I need comfort for what was in store for me in my childhood. One of the most scarring parts of my childhood was its instability. My family moved many times during my childhood. Between the ages of three to thirteen, we moved six times to be exact. We relocated from St. Joseph, Missouri to Harrisburg, Pennsylvania when I was three years old. From there, we moved to Indianapolis, Indiana when I was five years old. We transferred to another part of town in Indianapolis at age six. Then in third grade, at the age of eight, we packed up and moved to southern Indiana to a town called Terre Haute. Here, we would stay for five years, the longest I had ever been able to call one place home, until at the age of thirteen we relocated once again all the way north to Brooklyn Park, Minnesota.

Each move was progressively harder for me. As a child who was timid and quiet, I struggled with having to leave old friends and make new friends with each move. Shortly after moving to our new house in Indianapolis at age six, I came crying to my mother that I had no one to play with, and no friends in this new neighborhood. I was being vulnerable sharing with my mom how I was hurting.

Her response was, "Just go out and make friends."

There was no empathy there. There was no attempt to legitimately help me. As if it was that easy to make friends, especially for a naturally more reserved child. I sat there staring at my mom, stunned, feeling so unheard, invalidated in my fears about making new friends, and again, not comforted in any way. My mom just didn't get it. She didn't get me. Research by renowned author and trauma researcher, Dr. Bessel van der Kolk, has uncovered some surprising results in terms of what is the strongest predictor of future mental instability in children. Researchers initially hypothesized that hostile and intrusive behavior by a mother would have the most powerful impact on their child's future mental health. Instead, what was found was that emotional withdrawal and emotional distance had the most long-lasting effect on children's future mental instability. On the flip side, studies also reflect that having a good support system constitutes the single most powerful protection against becoming traumatized. By having a bubble of emotional protection, it's literally as if you grow a thicker skin to protect you from what life throws your way.

What is poignant to me is that my mother never had friends herself. I remember quietly remarking at this in my commonly contemplative way. I would witness other mothers congregating at school gatherings, at church, and in the neighborhood. They would laugh, plan get-togethers, and chat about life. My mother did not join in these conversational groups with other moms. My mother never had friends over to our house and never talked to them on the phone because they were nonexistent. She had no friends. She had no interest in fostering friendships.

I recall a couple of occasions where my dad would invite over a coworker and their spouse to our house, but these were typically singular occasions where I never saw them again, and they never visited our house again. Not only that, but my mom would bad-mouth the people as soon as they left our house, complaining about innocuous things.

"Can you believe they brought box-made stuffing instead of homemade?"

"Her hair was atrocious with all that hairspray!"

"That woman had the most annoying voice."

My mother was an enigma to me. On the outside, you may see her as a typical no-nonsense in appearance mom. She was of average height at five foot five inches and was always carrying twenty to thirty more pounds than she would have liked, mainly around her middle section. Her pants size fluctuated through my childhood from fourteen to eighteen depending on what new fad diet she was trying. Her Russian-German heritage bestowed upon her thick, nearly black hair with a slight wave from regular at-home perms. For most of my childhood, she wore a utilitarian haircut about four to six inches in length which she washed and air dried, doing nothing more in terms of styling. Her makeup routine was simple but consistent. To leave the house without makeup on was to appear ugly, unpresentable, and lazy in her mind. There was not a day that would go by that she would neglect to apply a simple face powder, blue eyeliner, and a swipe of Carmex chapstick. As I would later learn through her not-so-subtle judgments of other women, makeup made you look less old and haggardly, clearly a value she held dear. This air of judgment is likely what in part contributed to her repelling friendships.

Not until much later in my life did I realize, with a mix of sadness and epiphany, the basic understanding that my mother didn't have friends because she was not a friendly person. She did not reciprocate in relationships or put effort into friendships. She did not appear interested in other people's lives or provide validation in conversation with others. My mom did not possess the basic skills required for making and keeping friends. Instead in any given conversation with my mother, you would hear her finding something seemingly unimportant to complain about or expressing some sort of pessimistic opinion.

She could commonly be heard saying things like, "Who can stand this humidity, it never ends!" or "That neighbor's lawn is atrocious. Have you ever heard of a lawnmower?!" or "Get a load of that woman's annoying laugh."

The impression she blatantly gave others was one of a gossipy scandalmonger. The core attributes that are needed in building friendships with others, my mother did not have. The basic tenants of a friendship come down to trust, acceptance, and support. How would someone want to befriend my mother when it was clear she didn't accept people for who they were, would talk behind their back, and minimize others' concerns. What was peculiar to me, though, was that my mom never seemed to care that she didn't have friends. She seemed perfectly content carrying on with life the way it was and acted as if her way of life was superior.

More and more, isolation was the feeling I became all too well acquainted with while growing up. My core family of four didn't spend much time with my dad's extended side of the family. The reason my parents gave was that my dad's family lived far away from us. This was at least somewhat true. My dad's older brother, Ted, lived in Illinois for much of my childhood, and his older sister, Sarah, lived in Pennsylvania. But this physical distance didn't really seem like an accurate explanation for why we didn't see them as I was faced with contradictions from my parents. We would make the two-day drive to North Dakota to visit my mom's family, so I never understood why we couldn't do the same to visit my dad's family.

There were less than a handful of times that we saw my aunts, uncles, and cousins on my dad's side of the family as I was growing up, and this was largely for my cousins' weddings or a very rare holiday. One such rare holiday gathering occurred when I was around age ten on Thanksgiving, which my dad's brother, my uncle Ted, hosted at his house in Illinois. I was still only in elementary school, but I was struck by how antisocial my mom was during this event. My mom would throw sideways remarks to me throughout the day under her breath that she couldn't believe my aunt had taken shortcuts instead of making everything from scratch, remarking to me how her own food was so much better. It was like I was her confidant and she was trying to sway me into thinking badly about my dad's family.

In my head, I was thinking, "Who cares?!"

I was so excited to just get to spend a holiday with extended family that I couldn't have cared less about what food was served. Plus, my aunt and uncle were so warm in demeanor, embracing me with a hug and smile that said they cared about me. This stood in dramatic contrast to what I experienced with my own mother.

Over time, the puzzle pieces of the real reason we didn't spend much time with my dad's family came together. A story my mom let slip when I was in the room indicated that my parents had had my dad's mom over for Thanksgiving one year when I was really young and my grandmother had walked out per my mom's words, "in a huff" during the meal. I can only imagine what the reason for this was. My mom certainly wasn't someone who went out of her way to make others feel welcome. By the time I was hearing this story, my grandmother had passed away from complications of Parkinson's disease. This didn't stop my mom from telling stories about how annoying my grandmother was because once she found out that you had a certain interest area, she would only ever buy you presents centered around that theme. For instance, if she learned that you liked dogs, she would buy you all sorts of things with a dog theme in mind. Pictures of dogs, coffee mugs with a dog on them, paperweights of a dog. I didn't see what a huge deal this was. But it was clear to me from this impressionable young age that my mom didn't seem to know how to be respectful in interactions with others or be grateful for others. I long carried a sinking feeling that the real reason we didn't see much of my dad's side of the family was because of my mom. Either my mom didn't care to see them, or my dad's family really couldn't stand her so didn't make an effort to schedule visits with us. I often look back at what a little investigator I had become as a child, searching for clues beyond what was directly told to me to figure out the ultimate truth.

One truth I knew is that my mom came from a stereotypically giant Catholic family, born and raised in a tiny town in North Dakota with less than a thousand people in the population. She was one of nine kids. My maternal grandmother was one of eleven kids and my maternal grandfather was one of thirteen kids. Phew, can you imagine having such a huge family?! Family gatherings almost needed a stadium to accommodate everyone on my mom's side of the family. My mom had four sisters, two of whom she was closer to, and would talk on the phone with them as they still lived far away in their hometown in North Dakota. I was consistently struck at how impersonal and impolite their conversations were on the phone, though.

My mom would answer the phone, not with the traditional "Hello," or "Hi, how are you?", but instead with an abrupt, "What?"

In getting to know my mom's sisters further as I got older, I realized that most of her sisters shared many of the personality traits of my mother. They were also unaffectionate, blunt, socially unaware or inappropriate, and spent a great deal of time pessimistically complaining about various things of little importance. Was this just the way my mom was raised? Had she never known any other way to behave towards others?

In the summer before I entered third grade, my family took a routine road trip in our red minivan to North Dakota to visit my mom's side of the family. While there, we would indulge in homemade meals from our German and Russian heritage including fleishkuekle, knoephla, and borscht. My grandparents had a huge yard next to their house, decorated all over with foot-high farm-style ceramic lawn ornaments of chickens. It was very common because my mom came from a gigantic family, to have dozens of cousins over to my grandparents' house when we visited. One sunny, warm day during our visit, there were easily around twenty cousins over and we were in the yard playing TV tag. TV tag is one of the endless varieties of tag that kids make up; this version is one where you must quickly name a TV show as you duck down before you are tagged to escape becoming "it." While we were playing the game, my older cousin who was "it" came charging after me. I glanced back in what felt like slow motion, seeing with alarm that my cousin was closing in on me, and before I knew it, I suddenly tripped over one of my grandmother's lawn ornaments. It was a rooster to be specific. I landed with a crash right on my wrist and immediately felt crushing pain. I let out a blood-curdling scream and started crying.

My grandfather was the first one who reached me. Talk about a towering presence. My grandfather was tall and everyday wore suspenders to hold up his pants around his expansive belly. His voice was as loud as his exuberant personality. He certainly fit the bill in more than one way as the head of the family.

When he reached me after my fall, he firmly held my wrist in his hand, turning it all different ways, tugging, and pulling on it as he did, saying, "It's just a sprain. You'll be fine."

I was ushered into my grandparents' large house and was given ice by my grandmother. My wrist had swelled up pretty instantaneously and was so painful I couldn't bend it. I asked if we should go to the doctor and my grandfather was vehement that my wrist would be fine, and this wasn't needed.

A little background here on my grandfather that's pertinent. He was a well-known guy in their tiny North Dakota town for providing chiropractic care to the community. But here's the kicker—he's not a chiropractor. He worked as a coal miner before retirement. But adjusting people and acting as a pseudo chiropractor was his side gig. One he clearly had never been professionally trained to provide, but one he must have learned on his own. Because of this, my mom listened to my grandfather despite my continual expression that my wrist hurt really badly.

As expected, my mom doled out no comfort to me during this episode. Instead, she stuck me in my grandparents' living room with an ice pack and left me alone while everyone hung out outside. That night, I had a sleepover with my cousin planned at my aunt and uncle's house in the same town, and I barely slept a wink that night. My wrist was killing me, I couldn't bend it, and it continued to swell. In the morning, my dad finally relented and said they needed to take me to have it checked out. It turns out that my wrist was broken after all and I ended up in a cast for the rest of the summer. Worst of all, the doctor told me no jump roping until it was healed. As much as I was an often-sedentary child, preferring arts and crafts to sports, jump rope was the exception. I was a jump rope fiend, so to my eight-year-old self, this news was crushing. But even more so, I felt the added layer of hurt that my mom hadn't listened to me or trusted that there was more to it than a simple sprain. My dad was ultimately the voice of reason and I was thankful that at least one parent had taken me seriously. This wouldn't be the last time this very same thing happened.

3

Nothing is as Lonely as a Secret

Like any daughter, as a child, I looked up to my mother and wanted to feel that strong bond with her. I even went so far as to take on a somewhat motherly role with my own mom, trying to build her up or engage her in activities I thought she may enjoy. Some part of me wondered if deep down my mom had poor self-esteem. Maybe this was why she didn't have friends or why she constantly complained about her weight? I would swoop in and be the one to fix this problem. So, I became the cheerleader who would encourage her to try things she would say she couldn't do.

Like, "Hey, here's a new fun recipe we should try making together." Or "Let's learn how to knit together."

I even encouraged her to go back to school and enroll in college. My mom had never pursued higher education beyond high school and would often lament that she was too old and had too poor of a memory to succeed in college now.

She would always say no to whatever I offered, defaulting to a bland, "I'm not interested," response. I always felt the punch of the letdown that she wouldn't take my bait to spend time together. It was interesting and apparent to me from even a young age that as much as my mom complained about and criticized others, it was clear that her own self-worth wasn't high. She would often comment on how fat she was or how she had to buy a bigger size of clothing than she used to. Elastic wasted comfort wear was her jam. I tried

21

to be the encourager for her, but she always blew me off. Inexplicably, I still didn't give up trying to form a better bond with her. I naively thought that I could help her, and maybe even change the way she acted and treated others.

I didn't give up easily on my endeavor to connect with my mom. Perseverance is my middle name. Or you could call it stubbornness, but either way, I rarely give up once I set my mind to something. So, in addition to throwing out my ideas of activities we could do together, I would go grocery shopping with her, help her cook, and try to do things together to feel close to her. But time and time again, I couldn't help but see my mom's true colors. I couldn't help but see that my mother was not a kind person. I tried to ignore examples I saw that reinforced this, but in the end, I began to really see the type of person she truly was. I was saddened and embarrassed that she was so often just straight up rude and insensitive to others.

We did the majority of our household shopping at Walmart, and every single time a cashier would say, "Have a nice day," as we were taking our bags to leave, she would ignore the cashier's nice remark.

It didn't appear as though she didn't hear the cashier or that she was too shy to respond. Instead, it appeared like she didn't care enough to give the cashier the time of day with a simple courtesy of a reply.

I got into the habit (as a child no less) of saying, "You too," to the cashier as I felt embarrassed that my mom couldn't even reciprocate this simple kindness.

There were a plethora of other little things I noticed that my mom did or didn't do that reinforced that she was only looking out for herself and not others. She never held the door for others when going into or out of a building. She would constantly bad-mouth younger kids in a restaurant or church if they were making noise.

To myself, I would think, "Um hi, kids are noisy!"

She would also comment on other women's clothing or hair color and proclaim, "What were they thinking?" in her remarks on their looks.

She would condemn women who didn't wear makeup, even her own sister. I knew from a young age that I needed to make myself look the best I could to avoid her critical remarks.

I also quickly learned that generosity was not in my mom's wheelhouse. When people collecting food donations for charity would come to our door at home asking for canned goods we could spare, she would say that we didn't have any to share.

Interestingly, there were times when this happened that my dad would overhear and pipe in, "Oh wait, yes we do!" and then bring out a few cans to donate.

My mom knew we had enough canned goods to donate but chose not to. This was really an understatement. Not only did we have enough to share, but we always had MORE than enough food in our house. It was a common joke in my family that we were ready for the flood because my mom stocked up on food to the point that we struggled to have room to store it all. At times I thought that maybe this was the manifestation that my mom was worried that we wouldn't have enough food for some reason, but I didn't understand why she would have that concern. We had never gone without food. Even from stories that I would hear of my mom's childhood, they always had enough food as well. It seemed like her stinginess must be related to something else.

As I grew, I continued to construct an image in my mind and in my heart of who my mom really was. An even bigger shock that affected this image came when I was in fourth grade. I was sitting, perusing through old leather family photo albums with photos behind clear plastic sheets, where many of the photos had come loose from the glued backer. I was always a very sentimental child and liked to collect special keepsakes through the years to be able to look back on them later. I could spend hours looking through old photos in albums, trying to piece together some sort of history I could cling to and cherish.

In one box of albums, I came across a gold name plaque, like one that you would have on your desk at work. It had my mom's first name (which was a very unique name and uncommon name) with a last name I had never seen before. The last name wasn't my mom's maiden name and it wasn't our last name that we all shared. My mom had taken my dad's last name when they married so I was completely stumped. I showed it to my mom and innocently asked why it had a different last name. She quickly said it was nothing and then snatched it away from me with no further explanation. I was nine years

23

old, so still very young, but I was no idiot. I knew that you only got a new last name like that if you were married. I remember telling my friends at school what I had found and that I wondered if my mom had been married before.

Not once in the rest of my life though would I ever work up the courage to ask my mom or dad about it further. I think I was afraid of opening a can of worms I wasn't ready to deal with. I was afraid that this was some secret that maybe even my dad didn't know. I didn't want to rock the boat. Family secrets create invisible burdens. You can sense that they're there, but their hidden nature makes them impossible to process. I had enough instability in my life that I didn't want to create more. So, I just stuffed it down and tried not to think about it. But the reality is that I did think about it numerous times throughout the years, with an uneasiness I couldn't avoid.

It was also around this time that I got curious about my parents' wedding. I had found photos of their wedding day in an album and it struck me that the photos were fairly plain and unremarkable. There were only a couple of photos and they reflected my dad in a plain gray suit and my mom in a plain pink, knee-length dress. No fancy suit or tuxedo, and no big white wedding dress or veil. They had a maid of honor and best man present next to them but no one else. I had never even met the two people who had stood in as maid of honor and best man, which seemed bizarre if they had served this key role in their wedding. There was no family present at their wedding. Knowing that at least my mom came from a huge family made me puzzled why none of them were there.

My parents got married at the end of October and I was born at the end of May the following year. I ultimately did the math and realized that I was born only seven months after their wedding. I was old enough now to know that a baby needs nine months of gestation before they are born. I started to wonder if I was the reason that they had gotten married? Was it a quick, get married before people realized my mom was pregnant decision? Was I even wanted to begin with or was I an accident? I never felt comfortable asking these questions to my parents either though. I never felt safe enough opening up to my parents about my questions. But it hung in the back of my mind for years and years afterward.

Not only was any kind of open communication lacking with my mom, but the absence of appropriate boundaries in the relationship between my mother and me continued. Around the age of ten, while on another family vacation visiting my mother's side of the family in small-town North Dakota, we went to the mall in the nearest big city of Bismarck to do some shopping for clothes for the upcoming new school year. My aunt Sarah went into a dressing room with my cousin Harriet, who was a year younger than me.

My mom turned to me and said abruptly, "Why can't you be like Harriet and let me come into the dressing room with you?"

I was startled and embarrassed by this question. I had already begun developing by this age, was holding on to some extra pounds around my waist, and was uncomfortable with others seeing me naked. I was a preteen and definitely not secure in my body. I simply didn't understand why my mom didn't get that. I was nearing that teen age where girls just want and need more privacy. It felt like there was again something wrong with me because I didn't act the same way as my cousin. Instead of respecting my wishes, my mom made it into something that was wrong with me.

Peter Blos, the author of *The Adolescent Passage*, writes that this adolescent phase of individuation has been well accepted as a time when teenagers must disengage from their caregivers and establish a sense of self that is distinct. This process is proven to reduce psychological dependence on parents for approval, self-esteem, and emotional regulation. Yet again, I was made to feel that my age-appropriate needs were wrong by my mother.

Around this same time, my aunt Sophia and uncle Ben on my dad's side had sent me a diary as a birthday present. It was only about six inches by six inches in size and I saw it as a cute, compact secret keeper. As an introspective child, I enjoyed writing down my thoughts and feelings in the diary and felt secure in the fact that the diary came with a little lock to keep what I was sharing private. I didn't want my nosy little brother snooping and reading my cutesy cursive handwriting about my random school crushes.

One day, I was shocked when I stumbled into my bedroom finding that my mom had broken open my diary and was reading it. I was fuming with anger and asked what she was doing. She casually stated that she was cleaning my room and it had just fallen open. I of course knew she was lying and felt betrayed. I had literally caught her in the act and she still couldn't acknowledge her own mistake. That was the end of my journal writing days. I couldn't stand the thought of my mom, who I already felt like didn't understand me, reading my private thoughts and potentially misinterpreting them. With trust being such a core component of a healthy relationship, it's no wonder that the relationship with my mom felt doomed.

As much as on one hand I tried to forge a better relationship with my mom, there were just some things I could not ignore. Especially as I got older and started to reconcile the fact that though this woman was my mother and I was supposed to feel unconditional love toward her, I just didn't feel this way. Instead, all of her more annoying eccentricities became even more amplified in my mind. My mom would hide used tissues in the couch cushions that she would reuse repeatedly. She used a chip clip to hold her seat belt extremely loose, defeating the purpose of the seat belt, to begin with. There was her constant, ear piercingly loud throat clearing. For years and years, she had gone to various doctors per my dad's urging, to figure out what was causing it. No one could ever figure out a physical cause for it. Later as an adult, I did wonder if it was some sort of tic that she couldn't control. Harvard Health defines a tic as a sudden, rapid, repetitive movement or vocalization, and can be caused by an array of factors, though is most commonly associated with Tourette's Disorder. An example of a simple vocal tic is indeed throat clearing, which seemed to fit with what I saw with my mother.

The throat clearing, unfortunately, became a family joke. I think the persistence of this annoying behavior resulted in my dad trying to turn it into something humorous. My dad would joke that we would never lose my mom in a store or in a crowd because you just had to wait a few seconds until you heard her loud throat-clearing to find her. It was more accurate and effective than a GPS. It was like a beacon in the night. You could always find her because of this.

As I got older, though, I began to get embarrassed by this relentless throat-clearing. It was yet another thing that made my mom so very different from my friends' mothers. As a kid who wanted more than anything to fit in, anything that called negative attention towards me or by proxy to my family, caused anxiety and therefore was mortifying. At choir concerts in school, I would be standing on the risers singing and could hear the all too recognizable sound of my mom in the audience clearing her throat. In the video of my own wedding, you can hear in the background the unmistakable sound of my mom repeatedly clearing her throat. Maybe it shouldn't have bothered me as much as it did. But again, as the years passed, I was ever so hyperaware of the things that made me and my family different from others that I felt ashamed of it. Brené Brown, the renowned shame researcher, defines shame as "the intentional painful feeling or experience of believing that we are flawed and therefore unworthy of love and belonging." Because I ultimately felt that there was something inherently wrong with my family system, it caused me to feel a deep-seated shame that I was different from others and therefore lesser than others.

By the age of ten, my self-esteem was crashing and burning. Not only was I holding a few extra pounds around my own middle as my mom did as well, but I suffered from constant self-doubt and feeling less-than. Off-handed comments from my family stung and made me feel self-conscious. Not having a mother who I could turn to for support or who could provide reassurance that things would get better tarnished my self-esteem and made my self-loathing increase.

I was born with rather wild and unruly curly hair and was the only one in my family with this curly hair. I always felt like curly hair was my arch-nemesis. My mom did not pay attention to or style her own hair and was clueless about how to help me manage my frizzy pouf of hair. She would brush my hair while it was dry, which in the curly hair bible is a mortal sin. Not only that, but my mom told me I had too big of a forehead and needed bangs to cover it up. Bangs, when you have curly hair, are a recipe for hair disaster. They end up having a life of their own and I was constantly self-conscious about my hair and my forehead. Not until I went to college did I muster the courage to grow out my bangs and reveal the forehead I had long been told was too big. Guess what? My forehead isn't big at all and life was just that much simpler without having to constantly battle with annoying bangs. In the scheme of things, hair is at the bottom of the barrel in terms of importance overall, but it was just another drop in the bucket of an endless line of examples of how my mom's little jabs through her thoughtless comments stayed with me longer than they likely should have.

My mother wasn't shy about bluntly calling out what a big size in clothing I was now wearing as a pre-teen. She would continue to take me to the kid's section when it was clearly apparent that I no longer fit into those sizes anymore and needed to move up to the junior's section. It was like she couldn't really see the real me and was working off some unconscious assumption that I must still fit into these child-like sizes. This inability to understand that my body didn't fit the age-specific mold was somewhat ironic considering my mother also struggled with being overweight since I was born. She would often remark on how skinny she was before she had me. Throughout my childhood, she was constantly trying the newest fad diet and encouraged me to partake as well. She tried Atkins, Weight Watchers, and Slim-Fast drinks. She encouraged me to drink Slim-Fast drinks as a meal replacement when I was in fifth grade. This is where my own struggle with weight management began and how strongly tied my self-esteem was with my weight also ultimately began. Was my mom trying to prevent me from dealing with weight issues like she had? Was she embarrassed about me being pudgy? I had no idea. These little comments about my size and diet served to embed in my brain a pervasive worry about not being good enough.

It didn't help that my brother, four years younger than me, was naturally very thin. My parents often joked about how he could eat anything and never gain a pound. That comment was certainly never said of me. When I was eight years old, at my paternal grandmother's funeral, someone commented that I was growing up so fast.

My dad remarked with a boisterous chuckle, "She certainly never misses a meal!"

That comment stung. I remember glaring at him when he said it and feeling so self-conscious at a time when I should have been focusing on mourning my grandmother.

But this was the ongoing message I heard from everyone in my household.

As brothers tend to do, my brother found the right button to push when teasing me and it always centered on my weight. He called me "fat" honest to goodness nearly daily when I was between ages nine to fourteen. It cut me to the core and would more often than not trigger my tears to fall. It wasn't just that he said this hurtful word to me and the awfulness of that in and of itself. Adding fuel to the fire, not only did he do this, but often did so right in front of my mother. My mother completely ignored it and the resulting effect it had on me. When I would try to express my concerns to my mom that my brother was calling me fat and how it hurt my feelings, she would say it was his payback for how I picked on him, it wasn't that big of a deal, or that I just needed to let it go and develop a thicker skin. There was always a justification for why she didn't need to defend me and why my feelings didn't matter. The onus was on me to just deal with it. I would later learn that my mother's behavior was a subtle form of gaslighting.

Robin Stern, Ph.D., author of *The Gaslight Effect*, shares that the term gaslighting refers to a type of manipulation where the manipulator tries to get someone to question their own reality, memory, or perceptions and can be done intentionally or unintended. Whether or not it's intentional, the techniques a person uses to gaslight someone else include withholding (refusing to listen or saying they don't understand), countering (questioning the person's memory of an event), blocking/diverting (changing the subject or questioning the person's thinking), trivializing (making the person's needs and feelings seem unimportant), and forgetting/denial (pretending to have forgotten what actually happened or denying something they previously said). The consequences to the victim of gaslighting include second-guessing yourself, difficulty making decisions, ruminating about your own character flaws (like being too sensitive), confusion about your relationship with the gaslighter, feeling unheard, often apologizing to the other person, unhappiness, and feeling uneasy in the relationship.

Feeling alone and shamed for my feelings was an ongoing theme throughout the rest of my childhood. I was a timid, easily scared kid. There was a children's museum that we frequently visited in Indianapolis that had a beautifully intricate indoor wooden carousel. I was too scared to ride on

29

any of the ceramic horses on the carousel ride. Instead, I sat on the one bench amidst all the horses on the carousel by myself. No one sat with me. My parents would stand by my brother who bravely rode on the horses. I was also frightened of fireworks and when the Fourth of July rolled around, my family camped out on a blanket on the grass to watch the fireworks show at night. My mom, dad, and brother would be sitting together outside on a fuzzy warm blanket and I would sit by myself in the car where I could be protected from the loud firework bangs. Looking back, I'm struck by just how alone I was, both physically and emotionally. No one sat with me in these instances to comfort me or encourage me to be brave. I was simply an outcast and ignored.

With that said, my dad was certainly more capable and willing to provide emotional support to me than my mother. But my dad had his own issues that caused me great anxiety. He had this rageful side to his personality that seemed to sit just below the surface, waiting to appear. If my family was walking into a shopping mall and a car drove by invading what my dad must have considered our personal bubble, he would scream and bang on the hood of the person's car to communicate his intolerance of this behavior. He was never physically abusive in my home, but there were a few experiences that terrified me as a child. These instances caused me to question whether I could truly trust my dad for comfort and support, not knowing if his own anger and frustration would get the better of him or not.

One of the instances of surprising rage from my dad happened just as I started third grade and my brother started kindergarten. My brother was walking back home on the sidewalk by himself from a friend's house a few blocks from our house. As he passed a house just down our block, a man around twenty years old was standing in the front yard of the house and threw a six-inch-long knife at my brother. The knife landed sticking up in the grass. My brother, terrified, ran home as fast as he could and immediately came straight to me bawling. I hugged him and asked him what was wrong and got to the bottom of it. My mom was out running errands at the time and my dad was painting our house. After I comforted my brother, I told my dad what my brother had said happened. My dad immediately burst out the front door and ran down the street. My dad was an excellent, fast runner in his day, boasting a four-and-a-half-minute mile pace back in high school. He was gone in a flash. I had no idea what he was doing. He left me and my brother alone and the two of us started crying, only able to imagine what terrible fate awaited him if he was going to seek vengeance for my brother. In my head, I imagined my dad confronting this man who had thrown the knife and potentially putting himself in harm's way. Thankfully my dad came back safe and sound a while later, but no one ever discussed it again. He just pretended as if nothing had happened. I didn't want to rock the boat by bringing it up. My brother and I just intentionally avoided that scary house whenever we were out and about in our neighborhood.

Later, when I was in fourth grade, on Halloween, my brother and I had finished trick or treating and were getting ready for bed. We heard a scuffle on our front porch and my dad ran out to find some teenagers had smashed our pumpkins. What did my dad do? He took off sprinting after them, chasing them between houses and out of sight. He was gone for what felt like an eternity. I was crying, afraid that he would ultimately be hurt. After all, I had spent years and years in front of the TV at dinner time watching news of people being shot, stabbed, or otherwise maimed because of seemingly minor conflicts just like this. My mom just sat stoically, not appearing to be alarmed by this circumstance, and certainly not providing me any comfort either. My dad came back a while later and as expected, the incident wasn't spoken of any further.

About a year later, during the wintertime, my family was driving down a slushy street in a commercial part of town, when a large ice and snow chunk hit the front windshield of our red minivan. My dad immediately stomped on the brakes, pulled over to the curb, and jumped out of the car, taking off running after some teenagers who had thrown the ice chunk at our car as a prank. There we were, my mom, brother, and I sitting in the dark and in the cold in a strange part of town with no idea where my dad had gone. Again, I reacted by crying, worried that my dad would be harmed. My mom just sat there silently and calmly in the passenger seat, like it was just any regular moment. When my dad got back in the car, I finally confronted him and told him I was scared, and that he shouldn't do that again. I told him that he never knew if the person had a gun or something. He said he was fine and dropped it. I was left by myself to try to fill in the pieces, to try to understand what just happened.

Was my mom's lack of reaction a reflection of my mom just being so used to my dad's impulsive rage episodes that they didn't faze her anymore? Or was she in denial? Did this seem like a typical, justifiable action on my dad's part to her? I really had no idea what was going through her mind. But these moments were extremely frightening for me as a child. I was always in this state of hyper-alertness and worry that something bad would happen to my dad. Without my dad, if I were left with just my mom, I knew emotional support would be a hopeless wish.

4

Girls Just Wanna Have...

A sick child needs even more gentleness, compassion, and affection than a healthy child. I dreaded getting sick as a kid and throughout the rest of my life too. When I was sick as a child, I was ignored. My mom would make comments that I was trying to get attention or just being lazy, lying around. Clearly being sick was seen as a weakness by my mom. I recall a time when I was in third grade laying on our couch feeling like my head was going to explode and sweating profusely. I repeatedly told my mom that I felt awful and she told me just to lay there. Later when my dad got home from work, he recognized how sick I was, and finally took my temperature to find it was 104 degrees.

When I was sick enough that my mom needed to bring me to the doctor, and I was prescribed antibiotics, as soon as I started feeling better, she would stop giving me the antibiotics. She would then stockpile the leftover antibiotics in the medicine cabinet for the next time I was sick and give them to me without taking me to the doctor first to confirm that I needed them. Later as an adult, I learned what a huge no-no this was. But this was my mom's way.

She often talked about what a "quack" some doctor was and how they "didn't know what they were talking about."

My mom always knew better or at least believed she did.

As luck would have it, I ended up getting my first period when I was pretty young, at the age of eleven. Months later during the humid, sunny days of

July, shortly after I had turned twelve, I woke up with a terrible pain in my stomach. I told my mom and she said just to lay down. I laid a heating pad on my stomach to hopefully help the pain dissipate. My mom chalked the pain up to menstrual cramps, but I told her this pain was like none I had ever experienced, and I could barely move because it hurt so badly. Anytime I moved, shifted, or anything touched my stomach, shooting pain would hit and I would dissolve into tears. I barely ate or drank anything and didn't move from the couch for two long days. My mom largely ignored me, and I could sense from her that she thought I was being a baby or trying to get attention. Finally, after two days of this misery, my dad urged my mom to bring me to the doctor.

We had a very long wait sitting in the packed, stuffy waiting room at the urgent care clinic. I sat there slumped in my chair in misery as just even simply sitting upright caused horrible pain. I tried leaning back in my chair as much as I could to take the pressure off my stomach. All of a sudden out of nowhere, I got a very sharp, burning, explosive pain like nothing I had ever experienced in my life in the lower right side of my stomach. I screamed out in pain and started bawling. A nurse noticed me crying holding my stomach and said we could come right back to see the doctor. I was in excruciating pain and the doctor quickly decided that there was a strong likelihood that I had ruptured my appendix. Because they were only urgent care, they didn't have an ultrasound machine that they needed in order to diagnose if this was truly the issue. As a result, the doctor told my mom to take me straight to the emergency room. I hobbled my way to our car and had to sit with my seat reclined all the way back horizontally because of the pain, crying out in agony the whole time. Instead of taking me directly to the emergency room though, my mom brought me home, where my dad was playing basketball outside on our driveway with my brother. This was sadly before the era of cell phones and the many conveniences that they bring. My mom told me that she brought me home to ask my dad if he thought she should take me to the ER or not. What?? I sat there in the greatest pain of my young life and she was doubting whether I needed to be seen? Even after the doctor had explicitly told her my appendix could have ruptured. My dad said to take me, and he and my brother hopped in the van with us.

When we got to the emergency room, I immediately had an ultrasound completed and ultimately it was determined that I had a large ovarian cyst that had ruptured, and it was causing internal bleeding. The doctor said I would need to be admitted to the hospital as I may need surgery to stop the bleeding if it didn't stop on its own. I was terrified. Surgery?! I had never had surgery or had to stay overnight in a hospital before. I asked my mom if she would stay in the hospital room with me overnight. The thought of staying there by myself filled me with dread. She told me no, that my brother needed her and that I'd be fine. I was petrified about being all alone in the hospital through the night. But my mother didn't seem to comprehend this.

I had a terrible, fitful night in the hospital, as they had to continue to draw my blood every few hours to monitor my internal bleeding, so I got barely any rest. In the morning, my family came back and my dad presented me with a cute miniature Shar-pei stuffed animal he'd picked out in the gift shop that reminded him of our Shar-pei dog at home, named Wrinkles. It was a small gesture, and I was admittedly a little old for stuffed animals, but it comforted me. My mom did not hug or comfort me in any way. She just stood apathetically waiting. Luckily, by the morning, the internal bleeding has subsided, and I was able to be discharged from the hospital. I felt stung that throughout this whole ordeal, my mom hadn't believed the extent to which I was in pain and hadn't comforted or reassured me through any of it.

Later that summer, my brother, who was going into second grade at the time, and I were playing on our wooden swing set in our small backyard. We loved to challenge each other about who could jump the farthest off the swings. Honestly, my brother was tremendously more brave, adventurous, and sporty than I was, so often he won. This time, I had pulled off a whopper of a jump from the swing to the grass and I encouraged him to beat me. So, my brother leaped off the swing but slipped in his fall and landed on his arm with a crash to the ground. He yelped out in pain, so I guided him inside our house, calling for my mom to let her know he'd gotten hurt. When I explained that it happened from jumping off the swings, she glared daggers at me, and I sensed that she blamed me for what had happened. Even when we got to the doctor's office to have my brother's arm checked out, my mom specifically told the doctor that I had made my brother jump off the swing from too high. Again, it was my fault.

Sadly, we ultimately found out that my brother had broken the growth plate in his left arm and would need surgery to insert pins to hold it in place while it healed. I was devastated for my brother and felt guilty that it was somehow my fault. The guilt was there though I also knew in my heart that I had never wanted him to get hurt, and we were just playing as kids do. Thankfully he healed and recovered from the accident just fine, albeit with a double-jointed elbow as a memento. But even years later whenever my brother's accident was mentioned, my mom would continue to glare at me with the unsaid message that it was my doing. It was also baffling that my mom had not hesitated to take my brother to the doctor when this incident happened. She certainly did not leap to bring me to the doctor when I had broken my arm or when I had a ruptured cyst. It was these confusing instances that piled higher and higher in the back of my mind resulting in me feeling like my mom just didn't care about me.

Another startling boundary-crossing happened later that year when I was in sixth grade and my brother was in second grade. I still preferred to take baths at this age instead of showers. Our one and only shower in our house was small and rickety, whereas our bathtub was a quite large and spacious antique claw foot tub. I was now absolutely at an age where I didn't want anyone seeing me naked anymore. Unfortunately, that was a boundary my mother didn't hesitate to cross. She would barge into the bathroom when I was taking a bath to get something out of the cabinet, and I would be embarrassed at sitting there so naked and exposed in the tub. Worse yet, she would walk in with my brother in tow! I would quickly grab the nearest towel or washcloth to try to cover my private areas and emphatically told my mom I didn't want my brother in there when I was taking a bath.

She would remark, "Oh he doesn't know what he's seeing."

But that wasn't the point. I wasn't comfortable. Me. It was about my own comfort level with my brother seeing me naked. It brought to the surface all the feelings of embarrassment and confusion that she didn't get this.

I couldn't tell if my mom really was clueless in recognizing how others were feeling or if she just didn't care. I had begun to physically mature and develop already by the fourth grade and had hinted to my mom that I may need a training bra, which was mortifying in and of itself at that age to admit to her. My mom blew me off saying I didn't need one yet. But I was uncomfortable in my clothes without a bra and often hid behind layers and baggier shirts. It wasn't until sixth grade that my mom finally relented and bought me my first bra. Why did it take so long for her to believe me? Was she embarrassed by me? Was she mortified that I had begun to develop so early? Was she having a hard time accepting that I was growing up? Or did she just never really look at me close enough to realize that I was changing? Was she sticking to some preconceived timetable she had for when she thought it was appropriate to buy her daughter a bra? That's the thing about having a mother you can't open up to. You have to create the dialogues yourself. The default dialogue I came back to time and time again was that my mom didn't care. She would get around to doing things for me when she felt like it or couldn't avoid it any longer. My feelings were not a priority.

I learned early on that there was no such thing as getting positive attention from my mother. My mother didn't remark lovingly about the pictures I would draw for her, or if I did well in school. Later on, in high school, I proudly brought home a report card that most parents would be thrilled over.

My mom's only response was a flat, "What, one A-minus?!"

I remember feeling like I'd just been socked in the stomach. Never mind that every other grade on that report card was an A. She ignored all of that and poked at the one slight blemish instead.

This was really a trademark of my mother. Her bread and butter. Focusing on the negative. The worst part? If I ever expressed feeling hurt by her words, her response would be, "Oh I'm just kidding around," or, "Why do you have to take everything so seriously?"

Remember, trivializing the other person's feelings is a hallmark of the gaslighting techniques my mother fell back upon. It was always MY fault that I took what she was saying the wrong way. It never occurred to her that maybe SHE should change the way she spoke to her sensitive daughter.

Feeling rejected goes hand in hand with most of my childhood memories. When looking back through family photos, after my brother was born when I was almost four years old, I earned my place on the back burner. In almost every photo after my brother was born, you would also see me, not so subtly poking my head into the picture, vying for attention. Not only that, but my mom would make off-handed comments that my brother was such an easy baby and that I had been anything but. Apparently, I would cry and cry and always wanted to be held when I was a baby. Imagine, a baby that cries and needs to be held?! As far as I know, that's every baby that has ever lived. But for my mom, anyone who expresses a high level of emotions or appears in her eyes as emotionally needy is a pain, a nuisance, and less valued. Ultimately, that is exactly how I felt as I grew up. Less valued than my brother.

Starting when my brother was two years old until he was four, my mom forced me to allow my brother to sleep in my bed each night. My brother and I each had our own rooms and own beds, but my brother was afraid to sleep alone. So, my mom would have my brother sleep in my bed. I hated it because there was never enough space, so I would end up getting kicked and pushed around in my sleep. But I didn't have a choice. It was ultimately what my brother needed, and he was the priority now. Not me. It didn't occur to me until I was an adult how odd it was that my mom just didn't have my brother sleep in my parents' bed instead. Maybe this was my mother's way of realizing she couldn't comfort him and putting the onus on me instead?

To meet my mother is to quickly know that she has never given much thought to fashion. She proudly refers to the fact that she was a tomboy growing up. She happily wears cheap, poor quality, ill-fitting clothes, often from discount box stores. Growing up, these were the clothes I received as well. As I got older and entered the preteen years, I asked if I could get some clothes from stores like Target or JCPenney. These were hardly expensive department stores and, ultimately, they sold clothes for comparable prices to the ones my mom bought but had more styles that appealed to me as a preteen. My mom would exhale in disgust and exasperation saying my brother was more than happy to wear clothes from Walmart, insinuating that he was easygoing, and I was just being a pain. Never mind that to most, it would seem more than age and gender appropriate for a preteen girl to begin to care more about her appearance and the clothes she wears, more so than an eight-year-old boy like my brother. At the end of the day, my being a girl was just an inconvenience my mom couldn't tolerate.

In an effort to appear to be parenting my brother and me equally, my parents gave us new privileges at the same time. While this may make sense to do things this way on the surface, with my brother being four years younger than me, it repeatedly felt like I was getting the short end of the stick having to wait four years longer to get certain privileges. I felt inner guilt for even thinking this though. I knew not everyone in the world had a fraction of the things that we had, and I reminded myself to be gracious. But again, I couldn't help but see the inequities in my parents' treatment of me and my brother.

For instance, when I was in eighth grade, my parents let me have a TV in my room. Again, you've seen how important TVs were in my home growing up. At this same time, my parents also let my brother have a TV in his room despite the fact that he was only in fourth grade. There was no doubt about it that getting to have a TV in my room was special and I was grateful that my parents let me have it. But I still wondered why there was this inequality between my brother and me. Honestly, if it had just been this isolated incident, I would have been able to blow it off. But it was far from a singular incident.

Both my brother and I had the curse of crooked teeth. When I was a teenager, my dentist suggested that I could benefit from braces to correct my teeth being out of alignment. My front two teeth were crossing pretty significantly. These misaligned teeth were likely impacting the TMJ that I had also been dealing with. I would clench and grind my teeth so badly in my sleep that I often woke up feeling like I had a lockjaw. My mom told me that we couldn't afford braces and that was that. I was embarrassed and ashamed that we didn't have the money to afford braces but dropped it. I didn't want to make my parents feel the shame I was feeling. But not long after that when my brother's dentist told him he'd need braces, they followed through and got him the braces he needed. There seemed to be no significant financial change for my parents in the short span since I was told I needed braces, so it didn't make sense to me how we could all of a sudden afford braces for my brother. As it turned out, my brother, who also dealt with TMJ, found his TMJ to be completely resolved by the braces having corrected his misaligned teeth. I went on to struggle with TMJ for years, ultimately leading to me cracking a tooth in young adulthood. I finally spent the $5,000 out of my own pocket and got braces as a thirtieth birthday present to myself.

The inequities continued to pile up. When I was 15, I had diligently completed all my driving school classes, and behind-the-wheel training hours, and studied like a madwoman for my driving test. I was a book nerd and read the entire driver's manual cover to cover in preparation for the driver's test. On the day of my sixteenth birthday, I joyously jumped out of the car when my driving instructor, who could have been Jack Nicholson's twin brother based on looks, told me that I passed my driver's test and would get my driver's license. I had gently asked my parents for some time if it may be possible for me to get a car after I got my driver's license. Knowing that I was planning on continuing to be involved in many school and sports activities, and planned to try to get a summer job, it made more sense that I would have a car to get around in rather than my parents having to schlep me all over themselves. By that time both my parents worked outside the home, so they also simply weren't always home when I was needing a ride. My parents vehemently said no, that would not be happening. There was no explanation, it was just a closed subject.

Much to my surprise, about a month after I turned sixteen, my dad surprised me with a gently used, maroon inside and out, 1993 Dodge Spirit, a granny mobile that unfortunately stank of cigarette smoke from the prior owner. I was thrilled though. A car meant independence. I cherished that car for many years. It was clear that my dad had been the driving force behind getting me the car. It seemed apparent that my mom was not in great favor of this decision. I felt worried that my mom would hold this against me somehow.

I wish I could say I was surprised that when my brother turned FIFTEEN, my parents bought him a shiny gold barely used Pontiac Grand Am. Before he even had his driver's license. To add insult to injury, my brother ended up failing his driver's test four times before he finally passed and got his driver's license. He went on to have a number of car accidents which ultimately led to his car being totaled when he was eighteen years old. After the car was totaled, what did my parents do? They bought him a glossy red Mustang. I asked my parents point-blank why they had bought such an expensive car for my brother and they said that after he graduated from college, he would pay them back. But I knew that was a lie and he never paid them back for it. This was just yet another example of little jabs I felt throughout the years where my brother got what he wanted or needed. I felt such a mixture of feelings—confusion, exasperation, defeat, and finally, anger. At the same time, I felt the guilty pull of my subconscious for even having feelings of jealousy or noticing these inequalities. I told myself that I should just ignore it. Looking back, I can see how in some ways I had learned to gaslight myself. I was denying my own experience, trying to minimize it, so maybe it wouldn't hurt so much. If I could tell myself this reality wasn't happening, then maybe I could protect my feelings in some way. But when there are all these separate instances of blatant preferential treatment for your sibling compared to you, it becomes impossible to ignore.

Being someone who was fascinated with birth order and how it affected personalities, I wondered if this played a role in how my parents treated my brother and I differently. I was the oldest child. My mom was a middle child and my dad was the youngest in his family. My mom would regularly complain about how her parents had given her oldest and firstborn brother everything and how she and the rest of her siblings never got the same things as he did. My dad also hinted at how being the youngest was hard, especially having a sister who was the oldest child and feeling his parents treated her differently than they treated him and his brother. Did this lead to some conscious or subconscious decision to alter how my brother and I were treated? Was this why I was left to feel less than my brother? Were my parents harboring past resentment toward their oldest siblings? Or was it just as simple as gender bias against females? Sexism could also explain the blatant favoritism my parents showed my brother. I wracked my brain trying to make sense of my family dynamics. Maybe if I could figure out WHY this was all happening, I could also find a solution to repair it.

5

Nothing to See Here

My mother being different than other mothers sank in more and more as the years drew on. By the time I became a teenager, I began feeling a tremendous amount of embarrassment about this. When I invited friends over to my house, my mom was not conversational, didn't try to get to know my friends, or even try to appear friendly. She was aloof and standoffish. My dad, however, would greet them in a friendly manner and ask them questions to try to get to know them and make them feel comfortable in our home. But I still felt embarrassed and ashamed of my mother. The last thing any teenager wants is to feel different in a negative way. As a result, most commonly I would herd my friends into my house and immediately retreat to my bedroom and shut the door to create a safe haven to try to avoid my mother at all costs. This was my form of self-preservation.

Having learned at an early age that my mother was not someone I could turn to for support or comfort led to internalizing my feelings. Kids can process their difficult or negative feelings both externally and internally. Researchers Liu, Chen, and Lewis completed an analysis of the internalizing behaviors of children. External forms of processing often can include arguing, breaking rules, appearing moody, or quicker to anger. Alternatively, kids who internalize their feelings often experience negative thoughts about themselves related to their abilities, body image, or worth. For kids who internalize feelings, on the outside, they may seem to meet the expectations of going to school and even may excel there despite their internal emotional struggles. To the naked eye, they can present as if nothing is wrong. The downside of this internal battle is that it can lead kids who internalize their feelings to a heightened risk of depression, anxiety, somatic or physical complaints, and even teen suicide.

I struggled to cope with sadness and the emotional rollercoaster that comes with being a teenager. Not only did I feel like I couldn't show sadness in front of my mother, but I felt like I couldn't express joy or happiness around my mom either. This was due to my mom's tendency to either respond to me in a way that cut me off at the knees or she would just completely ignore my happiness.

Hearing a sneering, "What are you so happy about?" with an annoyed expression does not elicit a message that one wants to hear about your joy.

Neither does getting a blank stare from my mom with a flat facial expression when I would share something that I was excited about like an upcoming ski meet as if she was saying, "Big hairy deal. What's so great about that?"

Any emotion expressed to my mom was clearly unwanted. I learned it was best to be neutral. I needed to be Switzerland. Because of this, I became overly perceptive to others' emotional states and got big surges of anxiety when I could feel that someone was sad, mad, or even happy because I had the ingrained message in my mind that all feelings were bad.

My family's move to Minnesota when I was thirteen triggered a major low point in my life. In Indiana prior to the move, I was in the middle of junior high school, and prior to moving, had actually started to thrive, maybe for the first time in my young life. Most of the reasons for thriving had to do with school and friends. I had been actively involved in Student Council and was on the cheerleading squad (go Royals!). I had made some great friends and these friends were the essence of my support system. With my friends, I could laugh, cry, be myself and, to be frank, actually discover who I was. Before this time, I had felt like I was moving through life completely clueless and lost about what made me unique, or what made me special. I had never once heard my mother reflect on what she liked about me or what I was good at. This is something moms typically do that helps kids develop their identity.

It's common for parents to say, "You are so helpful with your younger brother," or "You are really good at math," or "Wow, you are an amazing artist."

I never heard these things from my mother. Without that typical behavior of a mother, I was left to figure out what made me ME on my own. Peter Fonagy, a clinical psychologist, found that parents who have high "reflective functioning," meaning they are able to consider what is going on in their child's mind and take a curious stance, bring clear benefits to their children, including promoting secure attachment, good social skills, the ability to "read" others, and an ability to regulate their own emotions.

In junior high I had started to really excel and shine in school, earning consistent As in my classes. By sixth grade, I was reading at a college level and in math, I was able to skip a grade level for more challenge. Teachers noticed my intelligence and gave me praise for my academic achievements. At first, I didn't know how to receive these compliments. I felt a mixture of embarrassment, guilt, and surprise. It was a case of imposter syndrome. Doubting your abilities and feeling like a fraud is a hallmark of imposter syndrome. Ironically, imposter syndrome is most common among high-achieving people, who find it hard to accept their own accomplishments.

My internal dialogue spouted when I would hear the teacher's praise, "They couldn't be talking about me."

I was nobody. I had no experience with people telling me I was good at things, so it was hard to believe when I first heard that I was standing out in the crowd. Slowly but surely though, my self-confidence had started to build with the help of these wonderful, motivating teachers. My friends also made me feel like at least during the school day when I was away from home, I had a place where I was cared for and seen. The school became a protective bubble for me where I could relax and let down my defenses.

Moving, in turn, resulted in losing my one form of support—my friends. My parents knew no one in the state of Minnesota and there was no family close by either. We were literally all alone, starting over in a brand-new state because of my dad's job transfer. No one had talked to me about whether I was OK moving. I was just told that this is what is happening. I felt like my own emotional welfare wasn't even on the radar when that decision had been made.

My memories from those first months were filled with enough tears to fill a swimming pool. I literally cried myself to sleep every night for the next nine months. I was seriously depressed, had no energy, overslept, and began contemplating suicide for the first time. I remember lying in bed at night praying to God to help me. I felt so very alone. Even though I had my parents and brother with me, my dad was busy with a new job, my brother was in fourth grade and certainly not at an age or maturity level where he was able to be emotionally supportive, and my mom...well my mom was oblivious as to what her daughter may need for support or that she even needed support, to begin with.

I tried to cope the only way I knew how. By changing myself to fit in. I realized there were many nuances within the Minnesota middle school social circles that were very different from the ones I left behind in Indiana. At school, I was like a sponge trying to soak in all the things I saw other teenage girls wearing or doing so that I could try to replicate them myself. I started straightening my hair to be more like the girls I saw in my new school. I would spend two hours at night with a plastic round brush and blow dryer, trying to tame my unruly curls. I ended up melting a few hairbrushes from all the heat I poured onto them. I ditched the old cheerleading sneakers that I loved and bought the same kind of shoes that other girls wore. I wore my backpack on two shoulders as the Minnesota trend dictated, instead of slung over one shoulder as was the custom in Indiana. Any little thing I could do to not make myself stand out and be different was the goal. I already had a Southern accent that was quite noticeable to my up-North Minnesota peers. One boy in class tauntingly called me "Indiana Jones" when I spoke, which just made me try all the harder to change the way I spoke. I wanted to fit in more than anything. It's not a surprise to think of a teenager wanting to fit in at school, but research from Anderman regarding the correlation between school effects and psychological outcomes during adolescence found that the sense of belonging and fitting in at school is even correlated with higher grades as well as the students' expectation for success overall.

On some level, my dad recognized that I wasn't coping well. He never said this overtly, but I could at least sense from his actions that he knew something was up with me and I got the message that he cared. When I was sobbing after another miserable day trying to acclimate to my new school, he would give me hugs and tell me it would be OK. I think at the same time, he was uncomfortable with my sadness because it accentuated the fact that he was the one who chose to have our family move to Minnesota so he could change jobs. I felt guilty for impacting his own feelings in a negative way, but I was also so angry that he had chosen to have our family move in the first place. It was clear it was a voluntary decision, not one he was forced to make. He had chosen to take a job transfer within his company.

To add insult to injury, I later learned that my parents had cashed in the savings bonds that were meant for my college fund so that they could pay for the move to Minnesota. As a result, I was solely responsible for funding my own college education. My parents didn't pay a dime for my undergraduate or graduate education. Wouldn't you know it, though, but they ended up helping my brother pay for his college degree? I never worked up the courage to ask why in the world they hadn't helped me at all. I knew it would be a fruitless conversation more likely to result in further hurt than anything else. Like most concerns, I had learned it was best to sweep it under the rug and just keep it to myself. I didn't yet have the courage to confront these issues head-on. Instead, I decided not to risk causing more conflict and angst by avoiding the issue entirely.

The passive-aggressive tendencies of my mother became more and more pronounced as I got older and I began to recognize these patterns for what they were. After our move to Minnesota in the eighth grade, about a month after the move, in the middle of social studies class, I was given a note from the school counselor asking me to go down to her office. I looked at the note in confusion as I wasn't sure what this could be about.

When I sat down in the school counselor's office, she told me, "Your parents have noticed that you have been sadder lately. Do you want to talk about it?"

I was horrified. I felt a mix of both extreme embarrassment and anger, that instead of broaching this subject with me directly, my parents would call the school counselor and have her do the job instead. She didn't say whether it was my mom or dad who had made the call, but this had my mother's name written all over it. I could imagine that perhaps my dad had communicated to my mom that talking to the school counselor may have been helpful. But with my mom being so uncomfortable with any sort of emotion, she just chose to skip the step of asking me directly if I might want to talk to the school counselor or express any sort of concern that she had about me TO ME directly.

I told the school counselor I didn't want to talk, and she dismissed me back to class. I was too stunned to share anything with the counselor. I should have been grateful that my parents recognized on some level that I needed help. Maybe if my parents had asked me directly or encouraged me to talk to the school counselor ahead of time, it would have felt helpful. But brought up in this fashion, it felt backhanded, like I was ambushed, and it was anything but helpful. I managed to get through the rest of eighth grade, primarily by keeping my head down and focusing on the one thing I knew I was good at, getting good grades in school. It wasn't until ninth grade that I finally began making new friends and slowly emerging from the cocoon I had wrapped so tightly around myself to protect me from all the many changes that came with moving to Minnesota.

Before I knew it, it was already the winter of tenth grade in high school. I had just begun getting involved in sports, finally had a good group of friends, and was feeling more adjusted to life in Minnesota. Then one evening my parents sat me and my brother down at the dining room table. I immediately knew something was up. I could always feel in the room when emotional tension was high. My mom wasn't making eye contact and my dad looked like whatever he was about to share was heavy on his shoulders.

My dad cut to the chase and said, "We're moving to Colorado."

I immediately burst into big sobbing tears. All I could think was, "Not again!"

I knew that I couldn't survive another move. My mom, without emotion, pushed a box of tissues toward me but just sat stoically in her chair. My dad went on to explain that the old boss that he'd had in Indiana was giving him a job in Colorado and that, "We need the money." You see, about six months earlier my dad quit his job suddenly due to conflicts with his boss. Despite his efforts, he had not had luck finding a new job to date.

Furthermore, good money management never seemed to be a strong suit in my family. I always heard very mixed messages about money from my parents. My mom would vent to me when my dad wasn't around that we "had no money" which led to me feeling guilty if I ever asked for anything that they would need to spend money on. My mom even hid away money from my dad in a hidden pocket of her wallet that she called her "secret stash." She told me about her secret stash, but it was clear I was not to clue in my dad to this fact. She would use this money when she wanted to buy something that she didn't think my dad would agree with.

Only later in adulthood did I recognize how dirty her sharing this secret with me felt. It was definitely crossing a boundary in the parent/child relationship. In their article about adolescents' experiences being caught between parents, authors Buchanan, Maccoby, and Dornbusch detail that when parents confide in their children in this triangulating fashion, they can create feelings of entrapment in their children. This is proven to be an extremely anxiety-provoking event to children due to the ultimate fear of their parents breaking up due to these secrets, which creates an attachment threat for fear of the loss of their family, home, stability, and possible source of affection.

And yet, despite the message I heard from my mom regarding money, there was always a ridiculous amount of Christmas presents under the tree year after year. I remember one year my brother counted that he had gotten thirty presents from my parents. We always had the nicest, newest model cars, and in Indiana even had a boat, which felt extravagant. Ultimately, because of these mixed messages, I never knew where my family sat with finances and whether we were actually secure or in trouble.

Back to the devastating conversation with my parents about moving to Colorado. I sat there looking at our Christmas tree with its overflowing pile of presents underneath it and said, "Then return all my presents!"

My teenage brain's logic said that if we needed money, they should return all these gifts and save our money, so we wouldn't have to move. My dad said in a resigned voice that it wasn't that simple.

With the emotionally dramatic flair that only teenagers can muster, I said through tears, "I'm not going!"

At this point, my dad stormed up from the table in anger and went upstairs. On the way up the stairs, he shouted, "Well, just blame it all on me then!"

I was crying to the point of nearly hyperventilating at this point and my eleven-year-old brother of all people was the one to come over to me and comfort me with a hug. I think my brother registered how big of a deal this was, especially to me, as he'd absorbed on some level how much I had struggled with our last move to Minnesota.

In the days that followed, I spoke to one of my friends, Maggie, about this situation. She registered to some degree what I was going through as she had also moved a couple of times in her lifetime and knew the toll it could take on a kid. She shared my concerns with her own parents and circled back and told me that her parents said that I could live with them for the next two years to finish up high school in Minnesota. Later, I boldly and emphatically stood up to my parents and told them that I was not going with them to Colorado and that I was going to live with Maggie instead. I was finally taking a stand and setting a limit on how much turmoil in my life I could take. It was the first time in my life that their reaction appeared like they may actually believe me and were taking me seriously. They didn't say this overtly of course, but I deduced from the look my mom and dad gave each other when I said this that it struck a nerve.

My friend Maggie's dad worked for an auto body company as a general manager. Maggie had continued to talk with her parents about my situation and mentioned to me that her dad had said that he'd be happy to see if there was a job within his company that could be a good fit for my dad. My dad worked in management and had always loved cars. Could this be a possibility? I crossed my fingers and hoped so. From there, Maggie's dad and my dad got into contact and as luck would have it, Maggie's dad offered my dad a management position within the company. To my great surprise, my dad took the job, and plans to move were abruptly canceled. Never did either of my parents talk to me about whether the decision to stay in Minnesota was at all due to me, but again, that was typical of my home life. A conversation about feelings, or really anything of substance, was a no-go. At this point, though, it didn't matter to me. I finally felt like I could breathe again without the impending doom of another move right in front of me.

6

If I Was Going Somewhere, I Was Running

As the remaining years of high school passed, I immersed myself in the hours outside of school in sports. I joined what some referred to as the holy trinity of sports in my high school: cross-country running, track and field, and cross-country skiing. It was called the trinity because once you joined one of these endurance-based sports, you inevitably got sucked in to joining all three. I credit my involvement in sports with what helped build up my self-esteem and self-confidence. I in no way considered myself athletic when I started these sports. I was one of the slowest people on the team in fact. But I poured my innate persistence into training and gradually got better at these sports and as a lucky bi-product, found a wonderful group of friends as well. Being in these sports throughout high school equated to around a hundred separate races and meets that I competed in total. My parents came to exactly zero of these events. I learned to be my own cheerleader during my races.

When going down a large downhill during a ski race, I would quietly reassure myself when feeling nervous by saying out loud, "You can do this. Stay calm. You'll be OK."

I learned how to speak the words I wished my parents could have said to me instead.

My dad at least had an excuse in that he was working later into the evening hours so logistically couldn't make it to my races in time. But my mom routinely got off work early and easily could have made it to my events. My mom would come to my choir concerts but frequently insinuated that this was because she had loved being in choir herself when younger, and it seemed to remind her of that joy in her youth. Again, the message I received was that the things that mattered most to me, like sports, didn't matter to her. Unless it was something she personally cared about, she couldn't trouble herself to make it a priority. Initially, I felt disappointed in seeing my friends' parents cheering them on at races and meets. But eventually, I became resigned to the fact that this was my life and just accepted that my parents wouldn't be there for me.

Throughout my teens, as I would inevitably experience conflicts with my mother, I found that when I would try to address them directly with my mom, I would immediately become flooded with emotions and end up crying. I think subconsciously I was reacting to the anticipation of being rejected by her, which caused me to begin crying right away in the conversation and then struggle to articulate and convey my message. John Gottman, a renowned relationship researcher, and psychologist describes this occurrence as emotional flooding. Emotional flooding hijacks the "thinking" side of our brains, the part that takes in the gray areas as opposed to seeing things in black and white. The thinking side of our brain considers both sides of an argument and stays aware of the real state of affairs. The problem with emotional flooding is that it causes the thinking side of the brain to shut down. Gottman goes on to say that this happens when our nervous system goes into hyper-drive because our internal threat-detection system alarm is going off, and we lose the ability to have rational thought.

Not only that, but my dad tended to jump to my mother's defense and end up raising his voice at me, which only exacerbated my tearfulness. Because this really wasn't a productive way to address problems, I began trying to write letters to my mom when we had a conflict. This way, I could thoroughly express myself without having to worry about sobbing so hard that I would get flustered and lose my train of thought. I also hoped that if my mom had the full information, maybe she would respond differently. Research by Paez, Velasco, and Gonzalez claims that people with a high level of difficulty describing their feelings showed a significant reduction in negative feelings after intensive writing. The hope here was that my mom may also be better able to put her own feelings into words through a sort of mutual journaling exercise with me.

My hopes were quickly crushed though, as I would get a scathing letter back from my mom with a defensive tone, deflecting blame back to me. The letters were fruitless and never ended up resolving things after all.

It's no wonder that as a teenager, I had a swell of emotions constantly just sitting below the surface, ready to blow. My friends often lovingly teased me that I would cry at the drop of a hat. If we watched a sappy movie together, I was often found blubbering away. Turn on *Steel Magnolias* or *Stepmom* and forget about it. I was a sobbing mess. It's no surprise that the mother-daughter unconditional love undertones in these movies would be particularly triggering to me.

When my friends and I would talk about one day going off to college or the last race of a sports season, my tears would inevitably start flowing. I was inherently sentimental about all these big moments. It makes sense to me now why this happened. Not only did I have all the teenage hormones flowing through me, but I also had never had someone who let me feel my emotions freely. I had learned for so many years through interactions with my mom to bottle up my feelings and push them down. So, when I was with friends, surrounded by people I was comfortable with, I could let these emotions out. At home was a different story.

The more I tried to resolve conflicts or find better ways to communicate with my mom, the more I learned that this was likely a doomed goal. In my junior year of high school, my mom abruptly out of the blue came up to me and told me that I should quit the cross-country running team and get a job. There was no explanation for why she felt I needed a job. It certainly wasn't like I was sitting around twiddling my thumbs with nothing to do. I was your classic overachiever teenager and was over-involved in everything related to school. By this time in high school, I was in three sports, choir, Treasurer of the National Honor Society, in the Student Council, co-chair of the prom decorating committee, went to 6:00 am swim practice at school three days a week, and was getting straight As in school, often neglecting sleep to cram my brain to maintain these grades.

Additionally, from what I had overheard from my parents at least, they were no longer concerned about money. I had gotten a summer job as a hostess in my friend's family restaurant the summer beforehand and had saved a good chunk of money that I was able to use as spending money when I wanted to go out with my friends. Besides all that, sports were one of the biggest things in my life that had improved my self-esteem and were also where I had met the best friends I had ever had. These sports were vital to me. It was like asking me to give up oxygen. Clearly, my mom had no recognition of that. I felt exasperated that she had so little understanding of her own daughter. I told her that I did not want to quit the team and asked if I could get a summer job instead.

Thankfully, and surprisingly, she relented with a brief and blunt, "Fine," before walking away in her typical huff.

What lingered though, was how tactless she was when trying to communicate with me.

I imagined how the conversation could have gone very differently if she would have opened with something like, "Jackie, I feel it's important that you help chip in more financially with things that you want. I know sports are important to you, but I'd like to talk about a way to fit in a part-time job as well."

This would have at least shown me that she had some sort of recognition of what mattered in my life instead of just blurting out that I should give up what was so important to me. But I was realizing that my hopes of healthy communication like what I envisioned in my head were only that, a dream. My mom was just not capable of communicating in this way. Many believe the hallmark of effective communication is effective listening. Being able to show the person that you have an open mind, value their perspective, and want to work together. My mother was always first and foremost focused on her own agenda and therefore, communicated that she did not care about my side at all.

Thankfully, I found other role models to fill in for my mom. I credit one of the biggest reasons cross-country running, in particular, was life-changing in how it improved my self-worth was due to my coach. Dave Bauer was the coach for both the cross-country running team and the track team. With his close-cropped gray hair, scruffy mustache, and thin frame, he had been a staple at my high school for as long as anyone could remember. One of the best parts of his coaching style was his emphasis on motivation and encouragement. He regularly gave out rewards to everyone on the team where the focus was on your own personal improvement, not where you ranked against your teammates. He rewarded positive attitudes, teammates who demonstrated great sportsmanship, and even those who added humor to the team. Not only that, but he handed out little motivational posters filled with inspirational quotes and encouragement. I plastered these posters over every square inch of my bedroom walls as a reminder to keep going even when it was hard.

Coach Bauer also came up with nicknames for everyone on the team. Mine was "J.D.," my initials at the time. This may seem like a minor thing, but I had never had an affectionate nickname anyone had called me before. My parents did not have any cutesy nicknames they called me by. I was always just "Jackie." Having a coach who thought I was special enough to bestow upon me a nickname was touching to me.

Mr. Bauer always made an effort to provide individual words of support to each of the teammates and knew just how to inspire you to do your best. I had never in my life had an adult role model like this. One who had known me for a relatively short amount of time but recognized in me something I didn't even see in myself yet. He knew I could do great things. And with his support and encouragement, I did. I improved each year on the team and even ran a varsity race during my senior year. I never would have thought a few years beforehand that I would be able to push myself in this way and achieve something I could be so proud of.

Throughout the remainder of high school, I tried to steer clear of my mom whenever I was able to. Avoidance seemed like the easiest way to avoid conflict and avoid emotional pain. I had developed a healthy-sized group of friends and was lucky to have opportunities most weekends to hang out with my friends, typically lounging at their house, going to the movies, or going to a parade or fireworks event in town. This practice of avoidance was self-protection for me. The less time I spent at home, the less anxious and down I felt. I didn't have to worry about an awkward and uncomfortable encounter with my mom.

One summer day after I had hung out with friends at a Fourth of July parade, I had come home in the evening with an awful stomachache.

I had mentioned this in passing to my mom (likely a mistake in hindsight), and she asked pointedly, "Well, did you drink something?"

I knew what she was hinting at. But Lord help her from asking me directly if I had been drinking ALCOHOL. She had to ask it in a backhanded way. I said I had drunk water and that was it. Because that was the truth. Again, I was pretty much as goody-two-shoes as you could be in high school. I so desperately wanted to be the epitome of "good" to get the positive attention of my mom and some sort of notice that I was a good kid. I never drank alcohol in high school. I never stayed out past curfew. The worst thing I ever did was tee-pee a friend's yard with toilet paper as a prank. I understand how parents have to be wary and suspicious about their teens drinking, but it still hurt that my mom was insinuating that the only reason I would have a stomachache was that I was drinking. I.e., I was doing something wrong. It was my fault. She didn't trust me. She didn't know my values and that I would not do that sort of thing. She never offered any sort of solution or help with my stomachache either. As always, I was on my own. In the end, I ended up kicking myself for even self-disclosing my stomachache as I felt I should have known the outcome that would be expected.

Sometime later, when I was in my late teens, I had come down with a terrible virus of some sort. In the middle of the night, I had woken up freezing and trembling from the inside out, but my head felt hot, and knew I must have a fever. My bedroom was in the basement of my parents' split-level house and our medicine cabinet with the much-needed Tylenol was upstairs. I painstakingly slowly walked upstairs but felt really dizzy and woozy. I remember getting to the door of the bathroom where the medicine cabinet was, and then everything went black. I had passed out and woke up on the floor.

I regained consciousness finding my mom standing over me saying, "What are you doing??" Not, "Are you OK?" or "What happened?"

My dad appeared a moment later and asked in a caring way if I was okay and then helped me back to my bedroom. I ended up having a fever of 103 that was making me semi-delirious. My mom simply wasn't capable of showing any sort of compassion or kindness in my moment of need. It never registered that way to me though as a teenager. I felt like I was doing something wrong. How dare I pass out. How dare I wake them up in the middle of the night. Children are naturally egocentric, meaning that they assume they are responsible for things that happen around them, including bad things.

My internal dialogue as such, read, "This was my fault. I was a nuisance."

I realized even more how it was best to fly under the radar to not attract the negative attention of my mom.

7

Apparently, Rock Bottom Has a Basement

It's a well-known fact that the one day a year when the most phone calls are made is Mother's Day. And most mothers deserve that extra attention from their kids. For me, I dreaded Mother's Day. The worst part? Picking out a Mother's Day card. I wanted to do the "right" thing by doing what everyone else did on this holiday. I would stand in front of the rack of cards at Target and feel like a phony. Before me were rows of cards expressing deep gratitude for the strong, loving relationship with their mother. Cards about how their mother was their best friend, their confidante, and their constant support. These cards were all lies for me.

None spoke to my mother/daughter dynamic professing, "Thank you for providing my basic physical needs but ignoring all of my emotional needs."

Hallmark hadn't hopped on that brutally honest card message train yet. Typically, I would default to finding the most generic card I could that said something to the effect of, "Thank you for being my mom."

Holidays and gift-giving times like birthdays and Christmas never felt exactly exciting. I only had one birthday party growing up when I was in the third grade, and in general, my family did not make a big deal of birthdays. Both my parents referred to birthdays as "just another day." There were always gifts because buying things was the only way my mother knew how to express love. However, buying gifts for someone requires a certain amount of insight into the person's personality and likes and dislikes. My mother did all of the gift shopping because my dad detested shopping. You can imagine what kind of gifts a mother bought a daughter that she really doesn't know. I was always polite and thankful for the presents I received, but none of the gifts were what I wanted or liked. She would pick out clothes that were in no way my style and often not even my correct size. Or she would give me things that were for much younger girls and not at all what I was interested in at the time. Sorry, mom, but most fifteen-year-old girls aren't thrilled to receive a Barbie doll or jump for joy in getting a kiddy coloring book.

The gifts only got worse as I entered adulthood. Despite it being no secret that I was a staunch feminist and had even minored in Women's Studies in college, she would buy me gifts so blatantly coated in stereotyped gender roles that it was sickening to me. I would regularly receive things like oven mitts, dish towels, and even a vacuum cleaner at my wedding shower—trust me, that was definitely not on my registry! My best friend often remarks to me that I hit the bullseye in picking out such great personalized gifts for people. This feedback is so appreciated because I do put a lot of effort into gift-giving. I really try to think about the person and what THEY would like or enjoy. My mother always seemed to buy things for people that SHE thought they needed. But again, missing the mark on gestures like gift-giving was just another sign of how my mother was very focused on her own beliefs, and not interested in the cares or opinions of me.

As I merged into adulthood, I developed strong opinions about many political issues. I went to a liberal arts college where I enjoyed being immersed in a community that discussed many hot-button issues going on in the world around us. My parents had always been staunch Republicans and instead, my beliefs were more in line with the Democratic party. I naively would try to start up conversations with my parents about upcoming elections and some of the political issues that were being talked about at the time. My internal alarm bells should have been ringing, warning me that this was a first-class ticket to shame town. I was chastened for voting for Democratic candidates and had to endure hearing my mom say what a "crook" or "idiot" the candidate I was voting for was. There was no ability to have an open dialogue about political issues without judgment. I was just instantly wrong and senseless for not agreeing with their political viewpoints.

When I found out that Walmart was using child labor in other countries for their products, I mentioned it to my mother, a devoted Walmart shopper.

She responded, "Well at least it means cheap prices for me!"

Ugh. Always the bottom line for my mom was what was in it for her. I felt so stunned by her response and just dropped the conversation in defeat. There was no point in bringing up subjects like this with her because there was no possibility of reciprocal conversation or exploration into our differing beliefs. After conversations like this, I would feel this self-loathing and anger towards myself for even trying to initiate conversations of value with my mom. Why did I keep opening myself up to these doomed experiments in conversing with my mom? There was no point. There was no chance of any sort of open, healthy conversation.

During the massive, life-changing transition to my freshman year of college, I slipped into another period of depression, triggered by feeling very alone. Moving away from home to a college where I knew almost no one was a trigger, reminding me of the past moves I had survived. I was naturally a quieter person in social settings and therefore I worried about making friends at my new school. In the first semester of college, I felt so brutally lonely. I couldn't call home for support and encouragement. My closest friends from high school were at different schools and though we kept in touch via email and occasional phone calls, it wasn't the same as having their face-to-face support and company.

On top of this, I had entered college pre-med, and my first semester was filled to bursting with a heavy load of classes and labs. I got my first ever D on a biology test and was beyond devastated. This was a major blow to my fairly fragile self-esteem. I wasn't ever super great at anything, except school. I had always gotten As and hadn't so much gotten a B on a test since junior high. I felt doomed. The depression I dealt with impacted the catastrophizing that I found myself swirling in. With the heaviness of the depression that I was dealing with, I struggled to concentrate on my schoolwork. My brain was often in a fog. I ended up consistently staying up way too late at night cramming my brain, trying to up my biology grade and keep up with my other classes. In hindsight, I realize that I had put a tremendous amount of pressure on myself with such a ridiculously difficult first semester of classes. I didn't have a mother who could help me process this or encourage me to go easier on myself though.

One week while I was away from home during my freshman year of college, my mom sent me an email saying that she and my brother would like to come to visit and take me out to dinner. This felt very uncharacteristic, but I was inwardly happy that she was making some effort to see me.

I met my mom and brother at Olive Garden, a restaurant in the neighboring town from my college. As soon as I sat down at the table, my mom dove in to tell me that she'd brought my brother so that I could help him with his math homework as he was struggling, and the concepts were over her head. That was literally the first thing out of her mouth when she saw me, that she wanted me to help my brother.

No, "How are you?" or "Are you doing OK?" or "I've missed you."

I felt duped and so let down. I thought she had a genuine interest in spending time with me but instead had just asked me to dinner so I could help my brother. I burst into tears and realized I needed a moment to compose myself after feeling affronted by my mom's admission. I slowly walked back to my car in the parking lot feeling stunned and humiliated. Once back in my car, I let my tears fall. My tears were not just over this one exchange with my mom. These were tears over letting myself get my hopes up that my mom was going to show that she cared about me. Tears of disappointment that this meet-up was instead more transactional, a means to an end of getting my brother the help he needed, thereby getting my mom what she needed. My tears were about all the bottled-up hurts that had accumulated one after another over the years.

After I had calmed down, I went back into the restaurant and told my mom that I was hurt that she would just launch right into wanting me to help my brother and not recognizing that maybe I needed a break and some support as well. She didn't respond to that, of course. She just ignored my comment as if it had never been said. Ultimately, I ended up helping my brother with his math homework because I did want to support him. I would have appreciated being given some sort of heads-up by my mom about this ahead of time. At least then I would have been able to realize her ulterior motive and reconcile my own expectations. I quietly ate my dinner and returned to my dorm, feeling misunderstood and unsupported again.

What I ultimately fell for was my mother's attempt at hoovering. The term hoovering derives from the vacuum cleaner corporation namesake. Hoovering in this context, however, speaks to the act of a manipulative person attempting to suck a victim back into the same dysfunctional relationship cycle by appearing that they have changed. The manipulator often taps into the vulnerabilities of their victim, such as a desire to be loved and accepted, and tries to hook them back into the relationship by showing that are willing to provide emotional reciprocity and show emotional maturity. However, the manipulator's purpose in doing so is solely for their own purposes and is often short-lived and quick to default back to old patterns. In my own case, my mother had appealed to my desire for attention and prioritization and had instead revealed her very different ulterior motive, crushing my spirits even further.

Towards the start of my second semester of freshmen year of college, my depression continued to spiral downward. I could often be found in a bathroom stall in my dorm or the stairwell of the dorm where it was private, crying uncontrollably. I was beyond overwhelmed. I decided to seek out counseling through the college counseling center. This time, unlike in eighth grade, no one had ambushed me into going to counseling. Because of this, I felt comfortable opening up. The therapist at the college counseling center helped validate the feelings I was having and helped me identify the tremendous pressure I was putting on myself to highly achieve academically. Together we explored what I could do to find a better balance. She encouraged me to join the track team that spring, both to have a physical outlet for my stress, and also for a fun activity that I already knew I enjoyed that could help me make more friends. Through my counseling, I also realized that I wasn't truly enjoying the pre-med classes I was taking and decided to explore some other possible majors. It wasn't just a matter of struggling to get the grades I had hoped for in these pre-med classes, but there was an inner tug in my heart telling me to find something I was truly passionate about to explore.

That spring I decided to take an Intro to Psychology class. I immediately fell in love with the field of Psychology. Learning about the inner workings of our brains and about how relationships affect us sparked a thirst for knowledge that I previously wasn't able to articulate. All those years of thinking deeply about relationships and feeling my feelings so intensely likely impacted my fascination with the field of Psychology, where I could put these innate skills to use.

In addition, I began to explore with the counselor the feeling that I wasn't happy at the college I had chosen. I explored transferring to another school that would better suit my interests and personality. Ultimately, I made a decision to transfer to a different college for my sophomore year. I yearned for a fresh start. And this time, it was a change of my own doing, not one that was being imposed by my parents.

I made it through that dreadful freshman year and returned to my parents' home for the summer where I would bide my time before the sophomore year began. I felt like I was just coming out of the cloud of depression and was feeling especially fragile emotionally that summer. I had not opened up with either of my parents about the depression I had dealt with or that I had been seeing a therapist while away at college. I just didn't feel safe sharing this information for fear of their reactions, particularly my mom's reaction.

Upon returning home for the summer, I had intended to get a summer job to save some money. But, finding a job when you're just looking for seasonal work isn't always easy. I scoured the newspaper each day (I'm dating myself here...this was sadly before the ease of finding job listings online) and tried to follow leads for jobs where some of my friends worked.

Each and every single day, when my mom got home from work, the first words out of her mouth were, "Well, did you find a job yet?"

No kind greeting or polite inquiry into how I was doing. Right to the point. No sugar coating it. Again, I didn't understand the reason for the pressure of finding a job. My dad was in a good steady job now and it was clear my family wasn't struggling financially. I personally didn't ask for much, and while I was looking for a job, I contributed around the house by cleaning and cooking. I still felt such pressure from my mom to find a job and it just wasn't happening as easily as I thought it would, despite consistent efforts on my part. I began to dread when my mom would get home from work and the inevitable question that she would ask me again.

One day, I just couldn't take it anymore. My mom had gotten home from work and again launched into asking me if I had found a job yet. I couldn't respond this time. I had reached my boiling point. There were no words left to say. I could have let that anger explode and started screaming, but I knew that would only trigger more conflict and make me seem in the wrong. Instead, given the choice to fight or flight, I chose to flee.I just walked right out of the house, got in my car, and drove down the highway away from my home. I was crying and feeling so hopeless and alone.

The dialogue in my head ran wild with thoughts like, "Why was my mom not able to show she cared about me? Why did I let her get to me so much?"

I felt anger at her and also at myself for allowing her to affect me so much. After all, I was the one who returned to her house for the summer knowing who I would be faced with each day. As I drove, I started imagining driving off the overpass of the highway and how all my pain would stop then. As I continued driving, this idea gained traction and I started getting scared that I would act on it. I didn't want to die. I just didn't want to have this emotional pain anymore. I just didn't want to have to deal with my mom anymore. So, I called my best friend, Becky, and asked if I could come over.

When I got to her house, I asked her if she wanted to go for a run together. Running was consistently a great form of emotional release and a stress reliever for me. People often remarked that we could be sisters as we were the same height with similar body composition and smiles. We would even accidentally wear the same outfit completely unplanned. Becky had always been my running buddy since I had started running back in high school as well. We often had heartwarming chats during our runs and often referred to our runs as "catharsis." In its essence, catharsis is a term for emotional release. Catharsis contains a powerful emotional component where strong feelings are expressed, as well as a cognitive component where you gain new insights as well. I hoped that a run, together with some anticipated catharsis, would help me feel better this time too. As we started walking down her driveway to begin our run, I burst into tears. I couldn't do it. I had no energy to run. I felt so defeated and scared. I admitted to her that I was thinking of killing myself and was afraid that I was going to do it. I trusted that I could be vulnerable with Becky in a way I couldn't be with my mother.

Becky took me back into her house and spoke to her dad. Together they asked if I wanted to go to the hospital for help.

I tearfully said, "Yes".

They drove me to the hospital and on the way, I just couldn't stop crying. I was nervous about my parents finding out what was going on with me. What would they think? Would they finally be able to help me? Would they be willing to help me? What if they just chastised me for feeling this way? There were so many worries running through my mind.

When we got to the hospital, they brought me into a room and a social worker met with me. The social worker emanated compassion and kindness. She was like the Fairy Godmother from Cinderella incarnate. I opened up about all the stress and depression I had been dealing with the past year as well as the pressure and lack of support I was feeling at home. I was crying and physically shaking so hard that she brought in a bunch of warm blankets to cover me with, but my shaking continued. The social worker asked if she could call my parents and talk with them about what was going on. I was tense and edgy about this, not sure what their reaction would be, but ultimately agreed.

About an hour later, my parents came to the hospital and walked into my room and awkwardly stood in the corner, with the social worker on a chair next to my bed. The social worker helped explain what I was going through and what I was feeling as I sat silently sobbing on the bed.

The social worker then paused, looked at my parents somewhat dumb-founded, and said, "You should go hug your daughter."

I read between her words the unsaid message of, "Um, hello, can you ding dongs comfort your daughter please?"

My parents had just been standing there twiddling their thumbs bewildered by me sitting there and it didn't even seem to occur to them that maybe

I needed some comfort. My dad came over and hugged me and my mom just patted me on the shoulder. That was it from my mom. The gentle, compassionate social worker helped facilitate a discussion of what I needed in terms of support. I was finally able to express that I needed more affection from them, to have real conversations about my feelings, and less pressure to find a job. Having the social worker's support by my side made me feel more empowered to speak this truth. My parents nodded along in agreement to make changes but didn't talk much. The ride home was silent. We never spoke of this night again.

I had no idea what my parents' thoughts and reactions were after hearing what the social worker told them about my concerns. Were they surprised? Were they bewildered? Were they angry? Did they understand or empathize with me? My dad seemed to understand on some level and took initiative by showing me more affection and initiating more caring conversations with me. My mom, on the other hand, did not show me any increased affection, didn't attempt to have conversations with me about my feelings, and continued to be the stoic shell of a mother I had always known.

Shortly after my hospital visit, I worked up some courage and asked my mom if she would be willing to go to family therapy with me. I hoped that having a third party who could facilitate more fruitful conversations between my mom and me would help, just like the social worker helped in the hospital.

My mom reacted by looking affronted and confused and said, "You can go if you want, but I don't need to go."

I felt shot down, and again as if my mom was absolutely clueless. She had no awareness of how she had impacted me and why going to therapy as a family could be helpful. My mom instead seemed to think that the problems all lay with me. Therefore, of course, I'd be the only one who needed therapy. I wasn't comfortable enough to bring up going to therapy as a family again and just dropped it. The one positive was that my mom stopped asking me if I had found a job yet and later on that summer, I did finally find a job, after all. But I counted down the days until I could go back to school and get out of my parents' house.

8

Them's Fightin' Words

Sophomore year of college at a new school was a breath of fresh air for me. I ended up at the same college my best friend, Becky, went to, and quickly made more friends and felt like the school was a much better fit for me. One of my new friends told me that she had worked at a Lutheran Bible Camp the prior summer and encouraged me to apply for a job there the summer after sophomore year. This sounded like a blessing in many ways. First off, the job sounded amazing. Being outside every day with other college-aged camp counselors and helping kids grow in their faith sounded like a dream. There was the added bonus that I wouldn't have to go back to my parents' house as I would live at the camp for the duration of the summer. It was a no-brainer. I was in.

When summer arrived, it was time to bring all my clothes and other odds and ends up to camp for the summer. My parents drove me there as my car was too small to fit the enormous plastic trunk that I would use to hold my belongings for the summer.

During the drive, my mother in her classic passive-aggressive manner, out of the blue said, "So, when did you stop eating?"

I had lost a bit of weight sophomore year which was honestly largely due to no longer struggling with depression, having more energy, and getting involved in the cross-country running team at college. I was by no means low weight or underweight though. This snide question from my mother caught me off guard and I didn't know how to respond.

I ended up just saying, "I didn't," and exhaled loudly in frustration.

She responded with a "Humph!" and the conversation ended as quickly as it started.

Internally, though, I was fuming. Why did my mother always have to start conversations in such a confrontational, negative way that triggered me to become defensive?

Why couldn't she ask in a respectful, curious fashion, like, "Hey, I've noticed you've lost some weight. Is everything OK?"

This would actually show me that she had some sort of concern for my welfare and show a curiosity about what was going on. But that was too much to expect from her.

I ended up working at a bible camp for two summers in a row and it was an incredibly good decision for my own mental health. Not having to be stuck in the same house where I was constantly bombarded with the emotional abuse from my mother was so freeing. I intentionally stayed at camp most of the weekends of the summer rather than going home on our weekends off to avoid seeing my mother as much as possible.

Later, when I was in my junior year in college, I continued to have extremely high pain associated with cramps during my menstrual period. I had dealt with this since my traumatic ovarian cyst experience at age twelve. These cramps were truly debilitating when they hit. I would curl up in my bed with a heating pad on my stomach and could barely move due to tremendous pain and nausea. My mom had always thought I was exaggerating the pain and ignored me when I mentioned it. Additionally, I ended up having a couple of other ovarian cysts that had ruptured in the years since my first. Thankfully these subsequent cysts weren't as severe or traumatic as the first. My doctor had told me that I could go on birth control to both help with menstrual cramps and prevent further ovarian cysts. I told my mom what the doctor had shared with me as I was still covered on their health insurance policy.

My mom immediately responded in an accusatory tone, "Do you NEED birth control?"

I could always read between the lines with my mom's abrupt, sparse, poorly thought out communication. I knew she was insinuating that maybe I needed birth control due to being sexually active. I stuck to the facts and told her no, that I needed it for cramps and ovarian cysts.

She responded with her classic, "humph!" and that was the end of it.

Chalk it up to another odd, off-putting interaction with my mom. Rather than trying to talk about the birds and the bees, my mom just had to slip in a sideways comment that made me feel interrogated rather than supported. Very typical. I told myself to just let it go.

As college progressed, I declared myself a Psychology major and excelled in the classes with material that I really enjoyed learning about. As I began acquiring knowledge about different mental health disorders, I noticed many similarities between my brother's behavior and Obsessive-Compulsive Disorder (OCD). I had long-lasting concerns about my brother's odd, repetitive behaviors, and bizarre grunting sounds he would repeatedly make at home. He didn't seem able to control or stop these behaviors himself. They also took up a lot of time causing him to struggle to get other things done. He would walk through doorways over and over again before he could move on with his next activity. He took hour-long showers due to many counting routines he engaged in while showering, causing him to be late for school.

I had mentioned to my mother my concerns that my brother may have Obsessive-Compulsive Disorder and my mom quickly responded with, "No he doesn't," in her typical dismissive fashion.

But the suspicion that I was right only grew from there. One time during that year, my mom had told me that my brother was failing his classes in high school because he was spending so much time counting the ceiling tiles during class, couldn't complete his homework, and cried himself to sleep at night because there were all these little sequences and behaviors he couldn't stop doing. My mom told me they were going to take my brother to see a neurologist because they thought he had Bipolar Disorder.

In my head, I thought, "What?!"

I was certainly no psychology expert at this point, but I felt confident that I had more education in this area than my mom did. For my brother's sake and welfare, I tried to trust my gut and assert myself to my mom.

My mom's plan made no sense to me. I didn't see any symptoms of Bipolar Disorder with my brother. He didn't seem to be showing any signs of mania, which is one of the hallmark components of Bipolar Disorder. Mania typically presents as a person feeling extreme euphoria, having very rapid speech, an abundance of energy and lack of need for sleep, a heightened sense of self-importance, being irritable, agitated, and distracted, or even experiencing delusions or hallucinations.

Furthermore, a neurologist wasn't who you typically saw for treatment of Bipolar Disorder anyway. I tried to reason with and educate my mom, saying that if that was the concern, a psychiatrist was a more appropriate provider type than a neurologist. I also gently explained that his symptoms seemed more consistent with Obsessive-Compulsive Disorder than Bipolar Disorder. A person with OCD experiences obsessions in the form of thoughts or urges that cause extreme distress and anxiety, which are then followed by compulsions, or repetitive behaviors meant to reduce anxiety related to the obsessions or prevent something bad from happening.

My mom told me they were going to the appointment she had made anyway. I threw my hands up in the air in frustration and finally just let it go, ending the conversation. I felt so infuriated that my mother would ignore my insights to the detriment of my brother. This wasn't surprising but it still stung.

Wouldn't you know it, but the neurologist ended up referring my brother to a psychiatrist where he was officially diagnosed with Obsessive-Compulsive Disorder. No surprise there, unfortunately. I hated the idea of my brother who I loved, struggling so much. I wrote him a letter empathizing with his struggles and even researched various celebrities with Obsessive-Compulsive Disorder, like Howie Mandel, to try to normalize what he was going through. I sent him research about treatment options for this disorder and tried to reinforce to him that there was hope for him and to not despair. It was hard being away at college while he was struggling so much, but he thanked me for what I did. I knew he was unlikely to get much emotional support from my mom, so I tried to compensate for her. I wanted to be able to help him. And I wanted to be able to help others.

Starting fresh at a new college ended up being a positive turning point for me as I felt ignited to become more involved with positive causes. By becoming involved with more activities on campus, I met more friends, and I also felt like I was doing something meaningful in the world. This helped lift my spirits and combat my prior depression. One of the groups I joined was Mission Jamaica. Over spring break, a group of students from my college would travel to Jamaica to serve at an orphanage that specialized in helping children with physical and mental disabilities. I was thrilled to get to be involved in this new experience.

The only downside to this mission trip experience was that it required a great amount of fundraising to raise a couple of thousands of dollars to afford each person's trip. The majority of people traveling on the trip raised the needed funds by asking family and friends of their family for financial support. I knew this was going to be tricky for me. Knowing that my mom's side of the family was not very generous significantly limited me. My dad's side of the family graciously donated funds to support me but his family is very small, so it didn't add up to enough to fully fund my trip. Given my parents really didn't have friends, that limited the pool of people I could ask for financial support. I participated in every other type of fundraising opportunity that the Mission Jamaica organization offered. I worked my tail off to raise these funds. But in the end, I was about three hundred dollars short. I didn't have this kind of cash myself.

I really didn't know what to do. I was so close to the goal and felt defeated. I swallowed my pride, held my breath, and asked my parents if they would be willing to pay the last three hundred dollars for my trip. I got the expected guilt trip from my mom and felt tremendously uncomfortable for asking them. She hemmed and hawed and huffed and sighed in response to my plea. In the end, they relented and gave me the funds. I agreed to pay the money back as soon as I had earned it. Mission Jamaica ended up being one of the biggest life-changing experiences I had had at that point in my life. I learned so much from the amazing children at the orphanage in terms of what was truly important in life. I was so grateful to be able to participate in this experience.

Imagine my disbelief when a couple of months later, my brother, who was a junior in high school, had persuaded my parents to pay for a plane ticket to fly him to Florida where several of his friends were going on a non-parent chaperoned trip at the end of the school year. The plane ticket cost seven hundred dollars. More than double the amount I had asked my parents to loan me. And they didn't ask my brother to pay them back the money for the trip. This wasn't a mission trip, just a trip for fun and leisure. I felt the ongoing tug in my stomach telling me that there was this uncomfortable inequality in how my parents treated me and my brother. I just didn't understand it. It hurt and yet I wasn't brave enough to address it with my parents. It felt like yet another fruitless topic to try to broach with them, knowing the likelihood of change was slim.

When it came time for me to graduate from college, I was understandably thrilled to have met this exciting milestone. But like most important events in my life, it was a double-edged sword. I was excited on one hand, but I dreaded the perceived obligation of inviting my family to participate in the event. More specifically, I dreaded having my mom there and the awkwardness that was bound to be present due to her social ineptitude.

After the graduation ceremony, several of my friends and I coordinated a potluck picnic lunch at a nearby park and invited our families to join. My mom brought an enormous two-gallon-sized Tupperware container filled with homemade potato salad.

She proclaimed loudly and arrogantly to the group that it was "THE BEST potato salad" and that people always loved it.

Trust me, it was nothing special. It was overfilled with mayonnaise and under-seasoned as my mom did not believe in simple seasonings like salt and pepper. I was embarrassed by her remark but just politely smiled along. She later remarked she couldn't believe more people didn't eat her potato salad as there was only a slight dent in it.

I prayed my mother didn't say anything else embarrassing and held my breath in hopes that she didn't spend the entire picnic enacting her trademark of complaining about menial things. The other parents congratulated all the fellow graduates on their graduation and enjoyed pleasant chit-chat with my friends. Several of my friend's parents asked me what my plans were for after graduation. On the contrary, my mother could be found drawling on about how hot it was, how it was too windy, and other topics no one cared much to hear and didn't inspire to initiate any sort of reciprocal conversation. My mom didn't inquire into what my friends' plans were. This would have taken an ability to care about others and show interest in others. Something she just couldn't do.

9

Do You Hear What I Hear?

After college graduation, I was fortunate to have the majority of my college friends live nearby, in, and around the Minneapolis area. Much to my chagrin, I felt I had to return to living with my parents after college as I just couldn't afford my own apartment yet. I had decided to go to graduate school to obtain a master's degree in Counseling. My broad-shouldered, curly-haired, happy-go-lucky boyfriend of two years, Tom, had also decided to move to the Twin Cities, Minnesota, to be close to me. He was actively searching for jobs and I hesitantly asked my parents if they would be willing to let Tom live with us for the summer after college while he looked for a job and saved up to get his own place to live. Much to my shock, they agreed. It seemed like my dad was the driver in this decision as he was always trying to look out for others, and I could tell my dad thought Tom was special.

Tom stayed in the small guest room in our basement that summer. This summer would be a massive turning point for me. It was the first time I received validation from someone else that something was off about my mother. And that validation came from Tom. As Bessel Van der Kolk, MD outlined in his book *The Body Keeps the Score*, "Feeling listened to and understood changes our physiology; being able to articulate a complex feeling, and having our feelings recognized, lights up our limbic brain and creates an "aha moment." In contrast, being met with silence and incomprehension kills the spirit.

One of the first things that Tom noticed was that my mother didn't put effort into showing that she cared about others. Tom quickly got a job and just so happened to get home from work each afternoon just after my mom got home from work, but before anyone else was home.

Each day, Tom would greet my mom enthusiastically by saying, "Hi! How are you?"

My mom would reply with a flat, uninterested tone, saying, "Fine."

That was it. No reciprocal, "How are you?" back to Tom.

Eventually, Tom told me he gave up and stopped asking how she was as the answer was always the same and she never seemed to show any interest in conversation with Tom. I was angry that my mom would treat Tom this way but resigned in that I wasn't surprised. I tried to make sense of my mom in my head. Was there some inherent lack of social skills with her? Did she not like Tom? Was she put out that he was staying at our house? Was she just that self-absorbed? I just ended up having more questions than answers though.

Tom was genuinely a saint and a blessing to me in so many ways that summer. Tom is by nature a super extrovert, great at making conversation with pretty much anyone to the point that I lovingly refer to him as a "schmoozer." He can make light of tense situations, has a gift for adding humor, and the best part? He's very in touch with emotions. He cries when he's really happy or really sad and isn't afraid to show it. He's very affectionate and loving and isn't shy about sharing affection with me. I felt like Tom in many ways acted as a buffer for me that summer with my mother. When there was awkwardness, he would provide a happy distraction.

Not only that, but he validated what I had shared in confidence with him about my mother. He saw it first-hand. He saw how she didn't express any caring gestures or affection to me. He saw how she complained incessantly about everything. He saw how she was very me-centric and didn't really have regard for others' opinions or feelings. He witnessed firsthand how much the TV was still the main character in my family system after all these years. Tom grew up with family dinners where the TV was not on or even in the same room as the dinner table. He saw how dinner time in my house was impersonal, quiet, and solely focused on a television instead of the people around the table.

It was then that I was finally able to put some confidence behind the feelings I had kept inside for so many years. This was a true milestone moment for me. Finally, I had someone who could see what I was experiencing. I wasn't just making this up. I wasn't just too sensitive. I wasn't misinterpreting things or taking things too seriously. The feelings of inadequacy and feeling unloved made sense. Tom's reflection back to me in being able to see what I had personally experienced was so gratifying.

Now with someone who could see what I had seen, maybe there was some hope of finding a way to change things with my mom. I still had this shred of hope that somehow, I could forge a better relationship with her. Though my hope wasn't huge, it was enough to keep me trying. But I was fearful and hesitant.

As young adults recently out of college, my girlfriends and I regularly spent a lot of time together. On one occasion, one of my girlfriends casually brought up that it would be really fun to do a mother-daughter trip together with all of our moms. I remember feeling like I'd just been punched in the gut by hearing this idea.

My initial thought was, "Oh dear God, no."

My friends were chatting about how much fun it would be to have all our moms get to know each other more and to do a bunch of fun girly-centric things together. Manicures, dinners together, watching movies. This trip sounded like a nightmare to me though. I'd rather have had my toenails pulled out with a pair of pliers. I knew just how the trip would go down if my mom came along. I would feel tense and uncomfortable the whole time. I would be on edge about how my mom would interact with the other women. I could just see her acting socially inappropriate, butting into conversations with some remarks criticizing others, and sitting around complaining about anything and everything the whole time.

I ended up saying something to the effect of, "I don't know that my mom would go for something like that," to my friends.

It was a cop-out because honestly, I had no idea if my mom would even want to go on a trip like this. But I knew I sure didn't. Thankfully, the trip never materialized, and I couldn't have been more relieved.

Though I hoped to change the relationship with my mom, I knew it would take time. It certainly wasn't going to help to jump into a mother-daughter trip with things continuing on the status quo. Bigger changes would need to happen first. I just didn't know how to go about it yet.

10

Will You Marry Me (and My Family?)

At the end of that first summer out of college, on a beautiful sunny day in September, Tom proposed to me and asked me to be his wife at the exact spot by a sparkly lake where we had previously shared our first kiss. I was beyond thrilled and remember the night after we got engaged, laying in my bed sleeping all of one hour as I was too buzzed with excitement to sleep, twirling the engagement ring on my finger throughout the night.

Interestingly, after the proposal, Tom told me how my mom had almost wrecked the surprise. Tom had sweetly told my parents ahead of time that he wanted to marry me.

It made my heart smile when Tom told me that my dad had proclaimed, "Nothing would make me happier."

My mom didn't have much of a reaction to Tom's news. Surprise, surprise.

Since Tom was still living with my parents that summer, he had told them of the day he was going to propose. On the drive to where Tom would later pop the question, my mom called Tom and was initially on speakerphone.

Tom had a premonition that he should take her off speakerphone just in time as she had blurted out, "Did you remember the ring?!"

Had Tom kept my mom on speakerphone, the greatest surprise of my life would have been spoiled. The thing is, this behavior of my mom was oh so typical. She was constantly reminding everyone in my family to not forget to bring something when they were leaving the house, reminding them of appointments, or reminding them to pack certain things when going on a trip. She constantly left Post-It notes around the house for my family with reminders of things to do. She never trusted that anyone could execute something without her reminders.

Months later, at my bridal shower thrown by my friends, I was tense as my mom had been invited to the shower. My friends had prepared a hilarious game to play at my shower modeled after Jeopardy and so named, "Tom and Jack-ardy." It was so creative, and my heart soared at the thoughtfulness they had put into it. The guests at my shower had to answer trivia questions about me and Tom to play the game. Unsurprisingly, my mom did not fare well in the game. She didn't know any of the personal details about my likes or dislikes, or even details about how Tom and I had met. Because she never asked me. She had never asked me those kinds of questions because she never even thought to. It hurt, but at this point, it was just par for the course.

As expected, when it was time to open presents at my shower, my mother's gifts did not fit the mold. As is traditional, Tom and I had set up a gift registry in preparation for our wedding. Our other guests chose gifts for the bridal shower from that registry. But my mom? No, she knew better what we would need than what we had carefully chosen. She gave me a vacuum cleaner and some hideously patterned oven mitts that were not at all my style. Was I grateful for the gifts? Yes, of course. Spending time and money purchasing a gift is certainly something I was thankful for. But in the back of my mind, was this ever-present reality that my mom just didn't get it. She didn't get me. She didn't get why it was more personal to buy things off the registry that was filled with items that Tom and I had hand-picked and believed we needed. Instead, she got me something I didn't want or need. Tom already had a vacuum cleaner. We didn't need another one.

Ultimately, I didn't want to be wasteful or ungrateful, so I kept those ugly oven mitts for years, but every time I used them, I was reminded of how they were what my mom liked, not me. Maybe I kept those oven mitts for so long as a symbol of the small seed of hope I also held onto that my mom would change. Years and years later I finally threw those oven mitts away and felt relief and satisfaction parting ways with that uncomfortable reminder.

After Tom and I were married, I made deliberate efforts to improve my relationship with my parents. Deep down, I really wanted things to get better. I thought that being out of my parents' house and not having to see my mother every day would naturally make things improve. I regularly invited them over to our house for dinner or to meet up for coffee. I really wanted to see if not living under their roof anymore could make a difference in the strength of our relationship. But I couldn't help but dread seeing my mother each time. I forced a smile, but it was awkward and unpleasant around her.

During one such meet-up for coffee, I was talking about my first job out of graduate school as a crisis counselor for an employee assistance program. I was remarking on how supportive my boss was. My female boss. My mom immediately launched into a speech about how she's never had a good female boss and how she thinks men are better suited to being bosses. She shared how her own boss thought she was "soooo great" because she had a college degree. My mom had never gone to college. This was clearly a sore spot for her, but instead of admitting that, she chose to find a way to make her boss seem like the one who was acting superior. I was flabbergasted at the blatant sexism coming out of her mouth! Actually, I could believe it, because I had gotten the implicit message throughout the years from her that men were superior to women.

But this time it struck a chord. I couldn't sit there anymore just silently ignoring her rude remarks. Much like the espresso machine in the coffee shop, I had to let out my steam before it would explode. I responded by telling her that what she just said was really sexist, that I couldn't believe she would say something so disrespectful, and that she knew, for goodness sakes, that I was a Women's Studies minor in college. How could she possibly say things like this to me and think I would be OK with it? After my response, my parents both sat there in stunned silence. They didn't respond to my comment but instead changed the subject. And just like that, what I said was glossed over and ignored. My mom never apologized for hurting my feelings. But again, she had never apologized to me for anything in my entire life. I was proud of myself for finally standing up for myself. I wished the reaction had been different but at least I could feel glad that I hadn't let her walk all over my feelings without consequence.

From early on in my life, if I told my mom that she hurt my feelings she would respond with something like, "You take things too seriously," "You need to develop a thicker skin," or "I was just kidding around."

It was always my fault that my feelings were hurt, never hers. Thinking back, I was a lot like a puppy who keeps getting kicked by its owner but continues to come back again and again, thinking and hoping that the outcome is going to be different next time. Her subtle endeavors at gaslighting me through the years had been effective in manipulating my feelings and making me doubt myself. Despite all of the hurt that I'd accumulated throughout my life, though, I still didn't give up on the goal of building a better relationship with my mother. Sometimes my own tendency toward persevering would lead to more bad than good. I don't know if I was a glutton for punishment, completely naive, or just so stubborn in wanting to make things better. Ultimately, I dreaded sharing any sort of news about my life with my mom. I especially hated sharing happy news because her reactions were always the opposite of what I hoped for and needed from her. I would hope for a smile from her at hearing my own joy. Instead, I got ambivalence, doubt, or completely ignored.

When I decided to run a marathon and told her, the first words out of her mouth were, "Are you sure you can do that?"

Her reflexive response was one of doubt. No response like, "Wow, that's great, you can definitely do that!"

I had, after all, run cross-country and track throughout high school and later again in college. I was in great shape and had run several half-marathons. A full marathon wasn't that big of a stretch. And you know what? I did do it. I followed a training program, put in my miles, and was ready for marathon race day.

But again, like an abused, naive puppy, I asked my mom if she and my dad would come to watch me run the marathon. The race was in a city about three hours north of where my parents lived.

My mom responded, "Well, we'd have to leave too early in the morning. I don't think so."

And that was that. No mind that my parents were naturally early risers and had driven long distances for various reasons before. The message that I heard was that my mom just didn't care enough to put in the effort to support me.

Confusingly, when I crossed the finish line of the marathon, there were my parents standing on the left side of the finish line. I was so shocked and bewildered and didn't quite know how to react. I wasn't sure if it was my dad's doing that had brought them there or what. My dad congratulated me briefly and then they both took off. That was it. The first time they'd ever seen me run a race in my life. I felt happy for that fact, but not quite the level of happiness I had hoped for or expected because it was tarnished by the original hurt of my mom not wanting to come.

My mom always seemed to have responses to happy events in my life that cut me to the quick and weakened the joy of the event with how she would twist things with her words. When I was ready to pick out my wedding dress, I idealistically envisioned that magical moment when your mom sees you in THE DRESS for the first time and cries tears of joy. I don't know why I somehow thought something like this was in the cards for me. I have always tried to be an optimistic person, so I think that aided in me ignoring all of the historical evidence contrary to what my dream was. Nevertheless, I invited my mom to come with me to go wedding dress shopping.

My grandma (my mom's mom) was in town that weekend visiting my mom, so she came along too. My grandma was really an older mirror image of my mother, both in looks and mannerisms. She was short and stout with curly white hair and a resting mean face. She was very quiet but also shared the tendencies of not showing much interest in others' lives, showing no affection towards others, and complaining about every little thing. The apple doesn't fall far from the tree.

So, there I was, in the dressing room, filled with glee to be trying on wedding dresses and dreaming of my wedding day. When I walked out of the dressing room in the various dresses I tried on, I was greeted by my mom and grandma with blank, uninterested expressions. There was no excitement emanating from them. They didn't express any positive remarks to me about how I looked, and I stood there awkwardly and uncomfortably in front of the big mirror not knowing what to think. I didn't like any of the dresses that night so put my own clothes back on quickly and left.

To my astonishment, my parents were willing to pay for my wedding dress, which I was grateful for. But on the downside, as a result, I was obligated to bring my mom along to my subsequent dress shopping excursions. When I found the dress that I fell in love with, I asked my mom if she was OK with spending the amount of money on the price tag of the dress.

She responded, "Are you sure you're going to marry him?"

I defeatedly sighed and said, "Yes."

But my heart just sank that she had spoiled this special moment for me with yet another inappropriate remark. What did she think asking such a dumb question? What kind of answer was she expecting?

"Oh, just kidding, this was all a prank! I'm not going to marry him after all!"

There was no logical answer I could come to.

Months later when the big wedding day came and the photographer was posed for the iconic moment when your mother zips you into the wedding dress and they snap the photo of the tear-filled moment, instead my mom yelled out, "Suck it in!" as she zipped me up.

There was no special photo of that moment. My face in the photo showed the disappointment and embarrassment I felt for the remark she made, right there in front of my friends and bridesmaids. P.S. there was no need to "suck it in." I had fallen into the trap many women fall into leading up to their wedding of watching my weight obsessively in the months leading up to my wedding and was honestly in the best shape of my whole life at that moment. I hated that her thoughtless comment brought back up those feelings of inadequacy that I had felt throughout my life. On my wedding day no less.

Ultimately, I loathed the fact that I let my mom get under my skin so incessantly. It felt like I had an obligation to include her in my various life events and one way or another she was going to find a way to spoil everyone. It never occurred to me that there was another option. I thought this was just what you did. Your parents would always be a part of your life and should be invited to all your big life events. This feeling of helplessness and dread that nothing was going to change kept growing, and I felt that I was stuck having her in my life forever. I couldn't imagine another option or a way out of this.

11

Don't Let the Door Hit You on Your Way Out

My mother's inappropriate remarks only continued with each new joyous event in my life. And with each joyous event, she shredded my happiness with her cutting words.

I told myself, "Just build a thicker skin." "Don't let her words get to you."

If I couldn't change her, maybe I could change me. But it was so difficult. I was still the sensitive person I had always been. I felt things deeply and that deep-down desire to be loved by my mom hadn't gone away.

When I found out that I was pregnant, Tom and I were about three years into our marriage, after a few months of trying to get pregnant. I told Tom that I just wanted to call my parents on the phone with the news rather than tell them face to face. I had an uneasy premonition where I just knew my mom would find some way to dampen the thrill of sharing this happy news. I wanted a quick escape option if I needed to abort the conversation by just being able to end the phone call rather than physically being in the same room as my mom. I wasn't just going to skydive out of the airplane without a backup parachute.

Sure enough, when Tom and I called together to my parents, we asked them to put us on speakerphone so we could tell both my parents at the same time. After we told them our joyful news that we were going to have a baby, we got the reactions I expected.

My dad's voice was filled with excitement and he said, "That just made my day!"

My mom's reaction? My mom said in a sarcastic tone, "Well, was it planned?"

What kind of a question was this? I was twenty-six years old. I had been married for three years and we had expressly stated to them before that one day we'd like to have kids. It's not like I was an unwed teenager. But this was just to be expected with my mom.

A socially appropriate response of, "I'm so happy for you!" was just not a possibility for me.

We hung up the call shortly thereafter and I dissolved into tears. Thankfully Tom was there to comfort me and understood why my feelings had been hurt.

I had long dreamed of becoming a mother. In my dreams, I had envisioned having a daughter that I could intentionally mother very differently than my own mother had. This would be my chance to develop a true, loving bond, and show my daughter unconditional support and caring. When I found out that I was having a boy instead, there was a moment of sadness I felt initially, thinking that I may never get that chance to create a better mother-daughter experience. But after that short bout of sadness, I realized that maybe God was giving me a son because it would be too triggering to have a daughter of my own. I could imagine the tremendous pressure there would be in making this new mother-daughter relationship as different as possible from the one I'd had with my mom.

Ultimately, I knew I was going to purposefully be a different mother than my own. It didn't matter if I had a son or a daughter. I went into motherhood with very different priorities. At least I knew that I had control over my own mothering style as opposed to the lack of control in changing my own mom's mothering style. My goals were to be open-minded to my son's opinions, show him I cared about things he was interested in, and above all else, show him affection and unconditional love and regard. I wanted him to have regular hugs and hear me say, "I love you," not out of obligation, but because I meant it.

Proper, healthy, respectful boundaries had never been present in the relationship with my mom, and they only got worse as time went on. In preparing for giving birth to my son, I knew that I needed to set some boundaries so I could enjoy those first tender moments with my new son without my mom tarnishing them. I politely and carefully told my parents that when I went into labor, I did not want them to come to the hospital until after my son was born and after we had called them saying we were ready for visitors. I knew that labor can be unpredictable and had no idea how it would transpire for me. I didn't want the pressure of having my parents right outside the door, or God forbid, in the delivery room with me when I may not feel ready for visitors.

When I was finally in labor, Tom texted my parents as a courtesy just to tell them that things were rolling. I was induced eight days past my due date and labor was long and arduous. It ended up taking thirty-three hours before my son finally greeted us. When I had been in labor for twenty-seven of those thirty-three hours, it was around 7:00 pm at night on a Sunday and Tom told me that my parents had just gotten to the hospital unbeknownst to him. He hadn't asked them to come. I was annoyed but frankly tried to ignore that fact. My epidural didn't ever take effect, so I was in tremendous pain throughout labor and honestly didn't have the emotional energy to worry about my parents waiting in the wings.

My beautiful son, Gavin, was born at 1:29 am on a Monday morning. Tom went out to the waiting room to share the news with our family. My brother had also joined the gathering in the waiting room and had apparently brought a video camera to document the event. Tom came back shortly thereafter saying my family wanted to come in right away. However, after Gavin was born, my body started going into shock where my arms and legs were shaking uncontrollably for forty-five minutes after Gavin was born. I also required stitches after childbirth which took another hour of time. When all was said and done, it wasn't until 3:00 am that I was finally stable and ready to snuggle my newborn boy. Tom had gone back out to the waiting room to update my family that I wasn't ready for visitors because I was completely exhausted. All I could think about was stuffing my face with something to eat and then getting any amount of sleep I could. I had been awake for over twenty-four hours and felt like it would be much more comfortable having visitors later in the morning after I could first get some rest. Tom came back saying that my family had left in a huff, with my mom saying that my brother had to work later that day and had waited around for nothing. I was so annoyed. I had literally, explicitly, told them not to come to the hospital until we had called them saying we were ready for visitors. But they had chosen to not respect that request.

Throughout my pregnancy, I knew that my intention was to breastfeed my son. I also knew that my own mother had formula-fed my brother and me. There was no judgment from me on her differing decision because let's be real—every mother needs to decide what is right for their kids. But I had this sinking suspicion that my mom was just waiting to spew judgment towards me for my differing decision from hers.

My breastfeeding journey was fraught with havoc, as I experienced lots of struggles, complications, and three bouts of mastitis breast infections as I tried to learn how to properly breastfeed. I delicately and vulnerably shared some of the struggles I was having when my parents were visiting.

My mom said, "I don't know why you don't just give him formula instead."

And she was right. She didn't know why I wasn't doing this. I tried asserting myself by sharing that breastfeeding was important to me and research showed it had many positive benefits for babies. She just blew off what I shared, though, and said again that formula feeding was far easier. That may have been right, but ignoring my own feelings and what was important to me, it sent the message that what I was doing was wrong. She didn't have the know-how that some things were really important for people, and this was an important issue for me.

The ignoring of boundaries continued after Gavin was born. My parents would just drop in to visit at our house unexpectedly and without calling first or giving us a heads up. As anyone with a newborn knows, having unexpected visitors is about the most unhelpful thing ever. It felt so jarring to have them just show up out of the blue, often when I was not showered and in the middle of trying to get Gavin down for a nap. The first couple of times this happened,

I gently explained that we needed for them to call us ahead of time and ask if we would be up for visitors as sometimes, we were trying to nap and catch up on rest or do any other number of things to keep our lives together with a newborn. My mom wasn't responsive to these requests and just seemed to brush them off her shoulder.

The next time it happened where they showed up on my doorstep, I put my foot down. I told her in no uncertain terms that I had overtly asked her to call ahead of time to ask if it was OK for them to visit and that right now was not a good time and that they could not come in. She looked affronted and angry and turned and left in a huff without another word. I felt good about putting my foot down though and keeping this boundary. And it worked. For the most part. A few slip-ups occurred but I kept strong to my boundary.

12

Gifts or Garbage?

One of the most bizarre occurrences with my mother was that each time she visited my house, she brought a plastic shopping bag filled with random things that she either didn't need or didn't like and pawned them off on me and Tom. Remember, that my mother only seemed capable of showing love through giving gifts, so I tried to rationalize this as an example of gift-giving. But it was peculiar in the method she went about it.

She would always say, "Oh I didn't like this pasta, so I thought you'd want it." Why she would think we'd like it if she didn't is beyond me. Or she would say, "We had this extra set of paper clips, so I figured I'd give it to you."

Not, "Would you like this extra set of paper clips?" She just assumed we would want it, instead of actually asking our opinion.

Most often when my mom gave us these plastic baggies, she was passing over to us various things she'd bought at the grocery store, tried, and didn't like, and somehow thought we'd want them. It was always the most random of things, and never things we actually needed or wanted. At first, we politely accepted them and thanked her for thinking of us. She would also bring us leftover food she had made and didn't think they'd be able to eat before it spoiled. But the thing is, as Tom and I grew our marriage, we found our tastes were far from the type of food my mom prepared. My mom liked to make lots of heavy stews, packaged processed foods, and hefty cream-filled meals consistently bland and unseasoned. I had grown up not eating healthy food as a result. TV dinners were a staple in my house, and as a kid, I often had slices of bologna, nachos, or toast with cheese on it for snacks. Not only that, but Tom had had gallbladder surgery and since, had to be mindful of avoiding heavy creams and fatty meats. Often the food my mom brought included just those things that he needed to avoid, which my mom was well aware of but seemed to ignore. We felt caught in a bind.

It was clear to Tom and me that we needed to set a healthy boundary here. When you find yourself being repeatedly mistreated, misunderstood, or disregarded, that can signal that a boundary needs to be put into place. By creating boundaries, you make it clear to the other person what behaviors are and are not acceptable, and you protect your own feelings from repeatedly being hurt, but you also provide a framework for a safe and functional relationship with the other person.

As time went on, Tom and I began to dread the obligatory accepting of the random rubbish she would bring us. Tom encouraged me to try to set limits by telling her that we didn't really need these things, and if my mom didn't like something that she had bought, she could just return it to the store instead of giving it to us.

When I would tell my mother this, she would respond with, "If you don't want it, you can just throw it away or give it to someone else."

The onus was always back to us, instead of recognizing that we didn't want these things to begin with and accepting responsibility for not bringing them to us, to begin with. We literally put up with this annoying habit of hers for years. In the scheme of things, it felt like a minor battle that I just waved the white flag at. There were certainly bigger fish to fry with my mom.

One of the most dumbfounding boundary-crossing disturbances happened one summer day when Gavin was less than a year old. We came home from an errand and walked into our fenced-in backyard to find my parents' old rusty patio table and chair set sitting on our deck. There was no note. There had been no phone call letting us know they were bringing it over, or you know, maybe asking us if we even wanted it to begin with. It was an old, outdated, shabby table and chairs, that in fact, we did not want. I was so taken aback and just plain mad. Mad about the fact that they would have the audacity to just drop it off at our house without even the courtesy of asking us first. This was our house, not theirs. We were not their garbage dump where they could just bring anything they didn't want anymore. Maybe I would have felt differently if this wasn't just yet another example of my mom crossing the line. If this was the first time something like this had happened, I could have easily reacted differently. But this pushed me past the breaking point. I called my mom and asked her why they had just brought this over without asking. She said she figured we'd want it. I told her that we didn't want it and that I was mad that she just assumed we would without asking. I told her I expected them to come to pick it up and take it off our deck. We weren't keeping it. I was so furious. She said fine and hung up. We never spoke of it again.

Once Gavin was in the picture and we were drowning in baby items covering every inch of our home and were feeling like we were bursting at the seams with "stuff," I finally told my mom to once and for all stop bringing us these plastic baggies of random things (read: crap). I told her if she really thought we would want something of hers, to ask us ahead of time before she came over, and I would tell her whether or not we actually wanted it. Again, she didn't listen to my request. She kept bringing her plastic bags of junk over to our house. And again, I had to put my foot down. I told her point-blank to stop bringing this over and that I was not accepting it, and she would need to bring it back to her house. I wasn't throwing it away or pawning it off on someone else. I just couldn't take any more clutter in my life. She still didn't listen though. Sometimes she would just passively and sneakily place these bags of nonsense in my house without even telling me, only for me to find them after she left.

Not only that, but she would also leave newspaper clippings randomly behind at my house when she left. And she would email me articles. These news articles were always about topics that she was trying to convince me about or that contradicted my own beliefs. She would send me articles about how almond milk was far inferior to regular cow's milk after I told her I liked drinking almond milk. Then she would send me articles about the best way to cook a chicken after I had made chicken for dinner with them. She even sent articles on weight management ideas. I always threw the articles away or deleted them from my email. She never talked to me face to face about them, so it felt odd how she went about it. They felt so inappropriate, passive-aggressive, and unwanted. Maybe if I felt emotionally close to my mom, I could have accepted them in a different way. If I had a closer relationship with my mom, maybe I would have viewed these as honest attempts to spark conversation between us or share knowledge. But since I alternatively felt no emotional bond with my mom and felt like she didn't know me at all, I felt affronted. The underlying message I got from these articles was, that you're not good enough.

I really, honestly, had been trying to make the most of our get-togethers with my parents. I would try to model a healthy relationship with my mother by asking her questions about her job or any other safe subject I thought could go smoothly between us. I would express empathy even when she went on her complaining rants and try to validate her frustrations. But the reality is that every time I knew I was going to be spending time with my mother, I could feel the tension creep up in my chest before the gathering. I even noticed myself getting snappier and short-tempered with Tom as a result. During the time spent with my mother, I felt on edge and like I could only share superficial things. Anything of substance or with emotional overtones would be ignored by her completely.

I remember in one moment of fortuitous vulnerability sharing that my best friend had experienced a miscarriage and she just flatly said, "Oh."

The conversation started and ended right there. I didn't know how to get her engaged in conversation.

Very commonly, the first words out of her mouth when I opened my front door to greet her would be a complaint like, "You'll never believe how bad our waitress was at Perkins."

No pleasant, "Hello," or, "Nice to see you."

In my head I would think, "My God, can she just stop complaining for two minutes or ever see something on the bright side?"

At the end of the day, I never enjoyed gatherings with my mother. It continually felt like it was an obligation to be endured and I always parted ways with her feeling worse rather than better. I felt so depleted. I continued to have this inner tension about my mother. I did feel a duty to try to be a good daughter and maintain a relationship with her and include her in my life. But on the other hand, I knew this relationship was not healthy and ended up in many ways doing more harm than good to my emotional state.

One thing that felt completely unexpected was that my mother showed affection to Gavin when he was a baby. She would light up at seeing him, tickle him, and read to him. What?? Who was this person? On the one hand, I was immensely pleased that she was giving Gavin the type of affectionate attention I hoped she would. But on the other hand, I wondered, why didn't she ever act this way towards me when I was growing up? Was there something wrong with me? Did she just not care about me or like me and that's why she never showed me affection? Or was she realizing the error in her ways in how she raised me and was trying to be a better grandmother? Internally, I hoped that having a grandchild had sparked a change in her.

Because of this reason, when my parents said that they would like to babysit Gavin, we opted to let my parents babysit Gavin on occasion. I was still nervous about leaving my beloved child in the hands of my mother. So, Tom and I made a point to only have my parents babysit when my dad would also be present, as I knew my dad would respect my wishes regarding how to care for Gavin. Deep down, I did truly want Gavin to have a strong bond with his grandparents but was certainly very protective of him, wanting to ensure my mother did not impact him negatively as she had me. I felt like there was some hope that having a grandchild had prompted some positive change in my mother and I wanted to relish in that.

What's interesting looking back, even when Gavin was a baby, is that there was a subtle peculiarity to my mom's interactions with Gavin. When my mom would hold Gavin as a baby, it often involved Gavin just slumped on her shoulder. She didn't put her hands on him while he snuggled on her shoulder. She didn't embrace him or rub his back. My mom just sat there passively, letting Gavin slump onto her shoulder. To someone else, it probably wouldn't have made much of an impact. But what I saw was that my mom was enjoying the snuggly affection from Gavin laying on her, but she wasn't reciprocating that to Gavin. She wasn't giving him authentic affection back. It showed me that at that moment it was about her receiving affection, not giving it.

As much as I had hoped that becoming a grandmother had changed my mom, I was sorely mistaken. Things did not seem to change in my interactions with my mom. When Gavin was just shy of two years old, I was hit with a terrible case of respiratory flu. It came on quite suddenly, and as is common, I spiked a high fever. I was very worried about Gavin catching it so in my desperation I called my parents and asked if I could spend a night in their guest room to try to spare Gavin from catching it. I certainly didn't want my parents to catch it either, so I asked them if they were comfortable with that, and they agreed. I had hoped that with my mother's increased ability to show some care toward Gavin, maybe this meant that she had opened her heart and would be able to show some of that towards me too in my time of need while sick.

When I got to my parents' house, they said they were going out to dinner just the two of them. I found it somewhat odd that they were leaving right as I got to their house. I traipsed to the guest room in the basement and it was absolutely freezing down there. I got all the blankets I could scrounge up but was still shivering from a combination of the basement being cold and having a high fever. In my semi-delirious state, I dragged the mattress upstairs to the other guest room as it didn't have a bed in it. I had no dinner and didn't feel up to trying to make something in the kitchen. So, I laid on the mattress on the floor of the upstairs guest bedroom where it was thankfully much warmer. By the time my parents got home, I had blessedly fallen asleep. I woke up in the middle of the night feeling on fire from my fever with a pounding headache. I felt like I could barely move. I knew I needed some more Advil to help my fever. My parents' bedroom was literally five feet away across the hall and I called out to them. No response. Then I called out louder. Still no response. Even louder. Still nothing. I was still so delirious and out of it that I felt like I could barely move. So, I lay there for hours, not able to sleep.

In the morning my dad checked on me and I told him how terrible I had slept and how awful I still felt. He said that he hadn't heard me calling in the middle of the night which wasn't altogether too surprising given he slept like a rock and snored on top of that. My dad asked if I wanted to rest on the couch where I may be more comfortable and helped me move over there. My dad had to work that day, so my mom was going to be the only one home. I was still running a high fever and asked my mom if she had any soup or juice in the house and if she might be willing to bring me some. She ungraciously and stoically brought me some and that was the only time she did anything remotely caring that whole day. I lay on the couch with a pounding headache and my mom proceeded to blare music in the kitchen and run really loud kitchen appliances like the food processor and garbage disposal. It felt like knives being driven into my brain and I wasn't able to sleep either as a result. I went out on a limb and timidly asked her if she'd be willing to turn down the music as my head hurt really badly. She huffed and turned it down only minutely.

Toward the end of the day, I called Tom and asked if he'd be willing to come to pick me up and bring me back home as I didn't feel with it enough to drive, and knew I wasn't going to get any better at my parents' house. I was so sad and honestly startled at how oblivious my mother was to my illness. I don't know what I was realistically expecting, but I had thought there had been some sort of shift in our relationship and felt like I should be able to expect more. I was obviously wrong.

13

No Response is a Response

As Gavin got a bit older, between the ages of three and four, Tom and I had added concerns about how my mom was interacting with Gavin. What we saw felt like foreshadowing that the relationship she had with Gavin was taking a turn towards resembling the relationship she had with me. It was around this time that my dad got a new job that required him to work a lot of nights and weekends. This unfortunately led to more get-togethers with just my mom. One time when my mom was at our house for dinner, Gavin took a tumble and fell down on our hardwood floors and started crying. My mom started laughing. Laughing! I was startled and stunned. Like a natural empathetic mother, I immediately went to Gavin, picked him up, and asked if he was OK. I told my mother point-blank that it was not appropriate to laugh. She continued to show that she was incapable of appropriately responding to emotions.

Regrettably, there were a couple of times when my parents were planning to babysit Gavin and then all of a sudden, my dad would end up having to work unexpectedly. This put Tom and me in an uncomfortable bind. Neither of us was particularly comfortable with only my mom caring for Gavin. Neither of us completely trusted that she would appropriately care for the emotional needs of Gavin in a way we felt at ease with. Alternatively, we did feel like my dad showed appropriate empathetic responses to Gavin and also trusted that he would always call us if for some reason Gavin was sad or missing us and needed us to come back home. We felt like my mom may ignore Gavin's emotions altogether. To be honest, we didn't feel comfortable directly broaching this subject. From our history, I knew that my parents would become instantly defensive if I at all hinted that we weren't comfortable with my mom caring for Gavin alone without my dad there. There were a couple of times that we ended up canceling our plans and forgoing having them babysit when we would find out my dad wasn't available after all. We didn't want to take the chance of having my mom care for Gavin solo.

The other reality was that both my parents were getting older, now in their sixties, and not as spritely as they were in their younger years. So, it just made more sense that they would be there together to back each other up when babysitting Gavin. Taking care of a young kid is no easy feat physically. And Gavin was a blue-eyed, dimpled, blond curly-haired ball of high energy. I did mention that I was more comfortable with both of them being present just in case one of them needed extra help caring for Gavin. I thought this would be an easier way to communicate that we felt it important for both of them to be there when babysitting. They did become defensive about this, saying that they were each physically just fine caring for Gavin independently. This wasn't really the honest truth on their part either, as my mom had a knee injury and couldn't sit on the floor with Gavin or chase after him, so there ultimately was a valid reason for our mentioning this.

The little voice in the back of my head started speaking louder to me that my mom's behavior towards me was repeating itself with Gavin. There were increasingly times when after my parents had babysat Gavin that I found out that they had let Gavin watch TV and given him candy when we had explicitly asked that they not. Gavin had shown signs of being extremely hyperactive from an early age, and we knew that a lot of screen time and sugar only exacerbated this. As a result, we intentionally and carefully limited both of these things. We would find out, from Gavin no less, after the fact that my mom had snuck him pieces of candy when my dad wasn't around or let him watch movies on her iPad.

I felt confused because when Gavin was a baby my mom seemed to have at least some level of appropriate interaction with Gavin compared to her behavior now that he was growing up. Later, I had a light bulb moment. I realized that babies require very little emotional processing and attention from us. Instead, babies mostly rely on adults to fulfill their physical needs of eating, changing diapers, and being held and put to sleep. You don't have to talk about emotions or resolve disagreements with a baby. But a toddler and older child require more than just those basic physical needs. Older kids need more emotional attention and conversational engagement. This was a struggle for my mom, and I think she reacted abnormally because of it.

When we would have my parents over for dinner, there were progressively more times when my mom would directly undermine our parenting in front of Gavin. Annoyingly, every single time my parents saw Gavin, they would bring him candy and many times, a random toy as a gift. It often felt like they were trying to buy his affection. It was certainly not the way we felt appropriate to build a bond with a child and only proved to teach him to expect something from them every time he saw them.

When we would tell Gavin that he couldn't have the candy that my mom had given him right away, or had to wait until after dinner, my mom would respond right in front of Gavin, "Oh one piece of candy won't hurt anything."

Can you imagine the message that a young child gets when hearing this? It turned us as parents into the bad guys and my mom into the good guy. I tried asserting to my mom when alone with her that as Gavin's parents, it was our decision when or if he was allowed to have candy, not hers. She just scoffed in response to my sharing this with her.

Feeling uptight and on edge around my mother was a near-constant feeling. When my parents were over for dinner at our house, my mom would stand over my shoulder and spew passive-aggressive statements my way, telling me that I was cooking the wrong way. She nit-picked everything I did. She would ask why I was cooking hamburgers for so long. Or why I didn't cook the pasta longer. She would comment on how she would boil asparagus, not saute it like I was. When I said I loved avocado, she would say it's gross. If I did anything or thought anything that differed from my mom, it was simply wrong. When I said I liked the color green, my mom said green was ugly. She couldn't just simply ignore it or keep her opinion to herself. This made me feel like I had to be on constant guard with what I shared with her, for fear of her expressing disapproval or disregard for my opinions or feelings. I wished that I was better able to just let her digs roll off my back, but I couldn't. I felt in a double bind constantly. The essence of a double bind is a situation where a person is confronted with two clashing demands or a choice between two undesirable courses of action. If I expressed my feelings to my mom, I was told that I was overreacting or too sensitive. If I kept my feelings to myself, I stewed in anger, hurt, and resentment. I couldn't win either way.

During this phase of my life, social media exploded. My mom had joined the bandwagon and created her own Facebook profile. I hesitantly accepted her friend request through Facebook, nervous about letting her into this circle where she could see more of my life than what I typically carefully chose to share with her. It was common for me to post photos of Gavin on my Facebook page, and my mom would comment with statements that rubbed me the wrong way. My friends would post comments on Gavin's photos expressing how adorable he was, and marvel at his beautiful baby blue eyes and scrumptious chubby cheeks.

My mom would post comments like, "He looks tired."

I wasn't sure what to do with that type of comment. Was it a judgment? Like, how could I ignore that he looks tired and not let him sleep instead of taking a picture of him? Who really cared if he looked tired anyway? As any Facebook or social media user knows, we shouldn't read so much into social media posts as they don't give us an idea of body language and other unsaid meanings behind the image.

When it was my birthday, my mom would post on my wall a bland generic, "Happy birthday," while my friends and even my friend's parents who I had gotten to know over the years, would post thoughtful, detailed birthday greetings remarking on and praising the kind of person I was. My mom didn't ever say things like that to me to my face nor on Facebook. I was often jealous when I saw my friend's parents raving on Facebook about their kids on their birthdays. Why couldn't I have that too? That pit of sadness in my stomach just ached.

Shortly after Gavin turned four years old, my mom's mom and my maternal grandmother died. She had been in worsening health for some time, so it wasn't a completely unexpected event, but certainly very sad of course. I certainly empathized with the grief my mom was going through and wanted to be there to support her.

Despite everything we had been through, I still repeated the mantra, "Kill them with kindness," in the back of my head.

I thought that if I showed her more kindness and empathy, it would somehow rub off and she would reciprocate it back to me. Subconsciously, I was trying to parent my mother the way I had hoped she would parent me. My grandmother had passed away in the cold of winter in December and the funeral was to occur eight hours away in my grandmother's small town in North Dakota. I took off work so I could fly in for the funeral. Tom and I decided that due to cost and the difficulty of traveling to a tiny snowy town in the middle of winter, Tom and Gavin would stay behind. I was feeling uptight and nervous about having to spend so much time with my mom's side of the family without the buffer of Tom there by my side. At the same time, I wanted to be there to comfort my mom. After all, I was trying to be a good daughter and demonstrate to her what empathy and care looked like. Deep down I thought that the more I poured out love and kindness towards her, then maybe one day I would crack through that hard shell and she would return it back to me.

At the wake the night before the funeral, we were at the Catholic church where the funeral was to occur. Down in the expansive basement of the church, my mom and her four sisters had gathered in a corner, and I was talking with my dad nearby. My mom and her sisters' voices got louder and louder as they started to talk sinisterly about my aunt Eugenia, my mom's oldest brother's wife. She was in charge of the coordination of the meal that would be held at the church after the funeral. Apparently, my mom and aunts had found out that she hadn't planned nearly enough food for how many people were expected to attend the funeral. Remember, my grandmother was from an enormous Catholic family, so herds of people were expected. My mom and aunts were going around and around saying horrible things about my aunt, in shock and horror at how she hadn't done her job correctly.

With it being a tiny town, there was no grocery store nearby still open and no other larger restaurants that could make food for the event with such short notice. I sat there listening to the annoying gossip mill run ragged for several minutes until I couldn't take it anymore. I spoke up and told them that I saw a Subway shop in town and wondered if they could make a bunch of sandwiches and deliver them for the meal after the funeral. It was like I was speaking Greek to them as my mother and aunts responded to my comment with silence, just looking at me dumbfounded, jaws agape. I called Subway myself and sure enough, they were able to take on this task for my family.

My mom and aunts relented in saying that this was a good idea. It certainly was not rocket science. But this was where my mom and my nature parted ways. When there was a problem, my mom complained.

My mom gossiped and said things like, "I can't believe it!" and placed blame on others.

For me, when there was a problem, you looked at your options and solved it. Dwelling on it and complaining and pointing blame at others wasn't productive. It wasn't going to solve anything. Not only that, but it caused more stress by letting situations grow to be bigger than they really were.

My mom unsurprisingly never said thank you to me for thinking of this solution. The closest I got was seeing that my mom had posted on Facebook about her daughter "saving the day" for her mother's funeral. It wasn't a direct thank you to me, but I at least took it as some sort of indirect praise. But really it seemed like my mom was trying to make herself look good by showing how great her daughter had been in this instance. It was really praise that was to be seen by her Facebook friends (of which admittedly there were few, and were mostly relatives), not for me personally. It rubbed me the wrong way in the end in how inauthentic it felt.

A few months later, my mom was babysitting Gavin without my dad, because again, my dad had ended up having to work last minute, and Tom and I risked what in hindsight was an ill-fated chance at letting my mom go it alone. I had been explicit, now that Gavin was getting more active and rambunctious, that if he accidentally got hurt or hit his head, even a small injury, to call me. I told my mom that I definitely understood that kids get hurt and I wouldn't blame her but wanted to know so I could decide if I wanted to come home to care for him. The night that my mom babysat Gavin, we got home when Gavin was already asleep.

When we asked my mom how things went, she said her typical bland response, "Fine."

The next morning when Gavin woke up, we immediately saw that he had a goose egg-sized bump on his forehead. When I asked what happened, Gavin said he fell and hit his head on the bench in our hallway. He said it hurt a lot and when I asked him if grandma had seen it happen, he said that she did. I was irate. I had been so specific that if Gavin got hurt to call me. As his mother, it was my right to know what went on with my son and to be able to decide if I felt it was worthwhile to come home and care for him myself after an injury. Not even to be told that this happened at all, and to have to find out from my four-year-old child instead was inexcusable to me. Mama Bear's anger had been ignited.

I ultimately decided that this incident needed to be addressed directly. I waited until I had calmed down and then called my mom directly. I expressed my concern that Gavin had been hurt and she didn't tell me about it. She said that she didn't think it was a big deal. I told her that to me, it was a big deal. I said that as his mother, it was my role to determine if it was a big deal or not and that by not knowing he had an accident, I would not be able to look out for signs of a worsening problem, especially with a head injury. My mom really didn't respond to this and tried to change the subject, so I ended the conversation as quickly as I could.

After this, Tom and I decided that we would absolutely not allow my mom to babysit Gavin alone anymore. From then on, if we needed a sitter, we would try to find another babysitter first. If we were unsuccessful in finding one, we would check with my parents as our last option. We also would double and triple-check that my dad would not have to work and could be there as well. Again, I somewhat naively felt like we could at least still help the relationship with Gavin and his grandparents flourish, even if the one between me and my mom was doomed. But I knew at the end of the day, I had to protect Gavin. That was the most important thing to me.

Additionally, my parents regularly asked if Gavin could come to their house for a weekend sleepover. My parents lived in a suburb of Minneapolis that was unfortunately heavily crime-ridden. Literally, just across the street from my parents' house, someone was shot and killed in the house. There were many burglaries reported in the area, including at another house across the street from my parents' house. Because of this, we did not feel at all comfortable with Gavin spending a night at my parents' house, especially without us present. I tried to respond to their request by telling them that I was concerned about the increased crime in their neighborhood and my parents' own welfare. I asked if they had considered moving to a safer part of town. They had hinted at wanting to downsize anyway since both my brother and I had now moved out of the house. I readily encouraged this for their own safety above all else.

My mom would also make comments to Gavin that I could tell made him feel uncomfortable. My mom would ask if he had any girlfriends in Pre-K or if he liked to chase other little girls around the playground. Good grief, he was five years old! For heaven's sake, let's not instill in him these heteronormative relationship expectations at this young age! Gavin would get embarrassed at the question and I would quickly change the subject to try to stop this uncomfortable questioning. At this time, Gavin's favorite color just so happened to be pink. My mom would remark to him that pink was a girl's color. We had already told Gavin that he could like any color he wanted. We were also intentional in telling Gavin that he could like or marry whomever he wanted when he grew up, a man or woman. It was very high in our value system to let Gavin feel comfortable just being himself, whatever that was. I hated that my own mother contradicted what impressions we tried so hard to instill in Gavin.

Ultimately, it was so hard for me not to be able to be my true self to my mother. I wanted to be able to be the person I felt I truly was—warm, compassionate, assertive in communication, a natural problem solver, and above all else someone who valued integrity and stood up for what I believed in. As a child and teen, I was frozen with fear of speaking up in front of others so was often disabled by shyness. But as an adult, I had worked hard to find my voice. Now I was not someone who when interacting with other people in my life would become passive, not speak my beliefs, or feel like I was walking on eggshells as I did with my mom. Instead, as I had become an adult, I had come into my own in terms of finding my voice, and when there were conflicts in other relationships in my life, I would try to resolve them head-on, rather than sweeping them under the rug and pretending they weren't there. I felt like a fraud in many ways for not being able to act the same way toward my mother. But time had told me that I just couldn't. It wasn't a safe relationship for me to be myself in. The consequences of being my authentic self were too great.

14

The Grinch that Stole Christmas

By the time Gavin had hit the milestone of turning five years old, Tom and I were feeling more settled in parenthood and like we could finally function beyond the basic daily to-dos. As a result, I offered to host Christmas at our house for the first time. With our extended family living far away, we spent 99% of our holidays with just my immediate family—my parents, Tom, Gavin, my brother, and his fiance, and me. I planned a beautiful home-cooked meal, decorated my house for the occasion, and was feeling in the blissful holiday mood leading up to Christmas day. On December 23rd, I spoke to my mom on the phone about something innocuous and she mentioned my Aunt Sarah was in town for the holidays. I was surprised and then immediately got a sinking feeling in my stomach. I just knew something wasn't right here.

I cut to the chase and asked, "Is she planning on coming to my house for Christmas?"

My mom replied matter-of-factly, "Well, yeah."

I told my mom that she had never mentioned this before now.

In her true "I'm always right" fashion my mom replied, "Yes I did."

I knew this wasn't something I would have just accidentally forgotten. Tom and I had expressed concerns about my Aunt Sarah on more than one occasion to my parents. She had come to Thanksgiving the year before at my parents' house, though I hadn't seen her for several years prior to that. She was on her third husband and Tom and I were incredibly uncomfortable around the newest husband. He chain-smoked and stank of cigarette smoke. I detest the smell of cigarette smoke and spent all of Thanksgiving silently gagging around him. Not only that, but he swore up and down in conversation and talked about inappropriate, uncomfortable topics when Gavin was right there. My Aunt Sarah also used lewd language around Gavin and talked about things that are not for children's ears. I had politely asked if she'd mind watching her language around Gavin but that didn't help. She also sat watching videos on her iPad throughout the Thanksgiving meal, which was very awkward, and frankly, she just plain made us uncomfortable. More so, I had opened up to my parents after Thanksgiving that we had been really uneasy around my Aunt Sarah and her husband, and they had said something to the effect that she rarely visited so it shouldn't be an issue again.

With my mom still on the phone, I bravely told her that I was upset that she had planned to bring my Aunt Sarah to my house for Christmas without even asking me beforehand. My mom responded back with an insistence that she had asked me before and that I was fine with it. (Recognize the gaslighting?) She went so far as to say she'd brought it up multiple times and even Tom was there when she'd brought it up. I told her that this did not happen because I for sure was not fine with it at all and never would have agreed to this.

My mom was blunt in telling me, "Well she's coming, so just deal with it."

This lit a fire within me. I was an adult. I was a 32-year-old married woman with a five-year-old child. I was tired of just silently dealing with my mother's disregard for my feelings, opinions, and convictions. I put my foot down. I told my mom that my Aunt Sarah was not welcome to come to my house for Christmas. I knew that Tom would firmly stand by my side in not wanting her there either. This was not just simply a preference for our sake to avoid her awkward behavior, but this was for our child's sake above all else. One thing we learned quickly upon becoming parents is that we had to make many tough decisions for our child's sake. We had to do what was right for OUR family. We couldn't just set aside our convictions and pretend we weren't uncomfortable with this idea. Could I have just let all of this go? Sure, I could have. I could have let my mom bulldoze me into agreeing to let my Aunt Sarah come. But I just couldn't do it this time. Enough was enough. I knew I needed to make a stand or this habit of my mom walking all over me would continue in perpetuity.

Upon hearing my stand that my Aunt Sarah would not be welcome at my house, my mom told me that she and my dad would not be coming either then. This really hurt. I shouldn't have been surprised by her immature response, but it still stung. Now my family, and my child, specifically, was being punished for her own mistake. Gavin was looking forward to spending Christmas at our house and hosting the rest of our family, seeing his uncle and grandparents on this special day. Tom and I had been excruciatingly careful not to negatively influence the relationship between Gavin and his grandparents. We never ever talked about the concerns with my mom with Gavin around. We really hoped that he would have a good healthy bond with his grandparents. The fact that my mother would let my son down in this manner was unacceptable to me. So, I told her. I told her how it felt like she was punishing Gavin for her own mistake. She quickly countered and told me it was my fault. I asked her if we could come up with a compromise. I asked if they would be willing to come over for even two hours on Christmas where we could have a quick meal together and exchange gifts.

My mom said, "No, if Sarah can't come, then we're not coming at all. We won't leave her alone on Christmas."

To that, I responded, "But you'll completely abandon us, and your grandson, on Christmas instead?"

My mom again threw it back in my face saying this was my choice and my doing. One of the other hallmarks of my mom's dysfunctional communication style is anytime she feels the limelight of blame is on her, she will deflect it by throwing your own past transgressions into your face. So, she dove into a dialogue about how several years prior my parents hosted Tom's youngest brother at their house for Christmas because otherwise, he would have been alone for Christmas. I said we were thankful for that, but that was a very different circumstance because I had ASKED HER if it would be OK beforehand. I gave her a choice. I respected her enough not to just blindsight her by having him show up at her house unannounced. At this point, my mom abruptly hung up the phone.

I called Tom and filled him in on what had just happened. Tom empathized completely and understood why I was so upset. He validated me in agreeing that my mom had not once brought up my Aunt Sarah visiting. He agreed that he did not want her in our house around Gavin either. I was crying at this point, thinking of having to break it to Gavin that my family had decided not to come.

The next day, my dad called me on my cell phone and my anxiety hit the roof as I answered.

There was no polite, "Hello," when I answered the phone, and instead, he said in a very gruff, angry voice, "We will be there tomorrow at 2:00 pm."

I was caught off guard and blurted out, "What?"

He said in the same furious tone of voice that they were paying for a plane ticket to fly my Aunt Sarah back to her home in North Dakota. For good measure, my dad said they couldn't really afford the plane ticket but that they had no choice. The guilt trip came through loud and clear. I responded in the question of this, asking why they wouldn't agree to just come over to my house for a short amount of time and then go back to their house and spend the rest of the day with my Aunt Sarah. My dad repeated that they wouldn't leave my Aunt Sarah all alone on Christmas Day. This made no logical sense to me at all. I was not aware of my Aunt Sarah being in some sort of fragile emotional or physical state where she as an adult couldn't be alone for a short period of time.

At this point, I said, "Well, I don't want you to come if you're going to be speaking with such hostility in your voice like this in front of Gavin." I told him that I didn't want to have this heavy tension in the air on Christmas day. I said, "We need to be able to come to some sort of healthy resolution because I don't want to ruin Christmas Day for Gavin."

My dad said they would act "fine" on Christmas, and it wouldn't be awkward. My dad's tone of voice softened, and I could tell he was trying to let go of his anger. I said that I was sorry my Aunt Sarah had got put in the middle of this situation, but that we had to do what was best for our family. My dad said he understood, and we ended the phone call in a calm place.

Christmas day came and to say I was tense was an understatement. Tom and I made a commitment to being gracious hosts and prepared lots of food for the occasion.

Tom and I greeted my parents when they arrived and my dad said, "Hi," with a smile, and my mom walked in and said nothing to me, diverting her eye contact away from me. Throughout the next several hours that they were at our house, my mom literally said exactly three words to me.

When it was time to exchange gifts, my parents opened their handmade hats and scarves that I had personally crocheted to match their winter coats. I had previously noticed that my parents never had warm winter hats and wanted to make something they could use but also hopefully like.

My dad appeared touched in opening the gift and my mom said one of the three words she said to me that day with a flat, "Thanks."

What did they give me? Again, my mom always did the Christmas gift shopping as my dad detests all forms of shopping. I opened my present to find that I had gotten a couple of dish towels and a packet of potato soup mix. That was my gift. A stereotypical good 'ole housewife present. I was internally affronted. Anyone who actually knew me would know this gift would offend me at the blatant message that I, as the woman and wife of the home, would want a DISHTOWEL for Christmas. I pasted a polite smile on my face and thanked them for the gift. I was trying to be thankful and grateful despite my internal feelings being quite the opposite. I didn't want to rock the very fragile boat we were already sitting on, so let this personal afront go. Tom made eye contact with me though and raised his eyebrows in a way that sent the message that he could tell this gift was offensive and not at all well suited to me. At this point in my life, though, I was used to not getting gifts from my mother that felt like they had been specially chosen for me. Again, in order to choose a touching gift that resonates with someone, you actually have to have some level of insight and understanding of that person. My mom just plain didn't know me. My own mother didn't have a clue about her own daughter.

After the Christmas season was behind us, Tom and I were looking forward to a ten-year wedding anniversary trip we had planned to Mexico in February. Escaping the Minnesota winter sounded heavenly. We had had this planned for several months already. We had spoken to my parents almost a year prior to the trip and they had said that they would like to take care of Gavin while we went on this five-day trip. I was hesitant to leave Gavin with my mother but felt much more comfortable when my dad promised that he would be there too. My parents agreed to stay at our house with Gavin while we were away so Gavin would have the comfort and predictability of his own house while we were gone.

After the blow-up at Christmas, Tom and I wondered if my parents would still be willing to watch Gavin for us for this trip, or frankly if we were comfortable with it. I called my dad and asked if they were still willing to do this for us. He said that they definitely were and were looking forward to it. I asked my dad point blank if my mom was willing to communicate with us about this so we could rest easy that Gavin was in good hands. My dad said that this would be no problem. So, Tom and I cautiously planned for this trip with a mix of excitement and trepidation about how it would go. We were worried about having to communicate what Gavin needed during our time away, especially with my mother, who had had zero communication with us since Christmas. To make things as easy as possible for my parents, and to make the transition as smooth as possible for Gavin, I printed out details of what his daily schedule was like, phone numbers for our neighbors and Gavin's pediatrician if they needed them, and made meals that I knew both my parents and Gavin liked, so they wouldn't have the burden of having to cook while they cared for Gavin.

I asked my parents to either call us or email us each day while we were away with an update on how Gavin was doing. My mom sent one very brief email on the first day of our trip with a very short summary of how Gavin was doing.

Her email basically amounted to a raving description stating, "He was doing fine."

For an anxiety-prone mother like myself, this told me exactly nothing about how Gavin was doing. The next day there was no email or phone call from my parents. I called and reached my mom, but the phone reception in the area we were staying was horrible, and it was basically impossible to understand each other on the phone. I sent an email asking for more detail about how Gavin was doing, asking some specific questions about how he was sleeping and eating. My mom again replied to my email saying Gavin was "fine" and blew off responses to the other questions I had asked. I was nervous and uncomfortable and questioned why I had agreed to leave Gavin in her hands. I reminded myself that my dad was there too, and though he really didn't email because technology of any kind was not his friend, he would make sure they kept to Gavin's schedule and make sure his emotional needs were met in a way I knew my mother couldn't.

After we returned from our trip to Mexico, we thanked my parents profusely for caring for Gavin in our absence. We brought them thank you gifts, knowing my parents were always very gift-focused in how they showed love. My dad said thank you for receiving these gifts and my mom said nothing. After that, my parents did not speak to me for several months. I also chose not to initiate contact with them either because I felt I needed some space to wrap my head around the relationship with my mother. I still felt really angry about the incident at Christmas and the ongoing awkwardness when interacting with her.

In early August, my dad broke the silence and reached out to invite us to a barbecue at their house. This was the first contact we had with my parents since February. This was the longest I had ever gone without some form of communication from them. We came to their house, and it was again very awkward around my mother. She barely spoke to me the entire time we were there, so I tried distracting myself by playing with Gavin in the backyard. My dad was friendly and conversational and that was a relief. My brother's wedding was coming up the next month in September and I vowed to just try to keep the peace until the wedding was over. The last thing I wanted to do was put any sort of damper on my brother's special day.

I was looking forward to my brother's wedding day because I would get to see my dad's older sister, Sophia, and her husband, my uncle Ben. My aunt and uncle were very special to me, despite not getting to physically see them face to face very often as they lived in Pennsylvania. They had never had children of their own but were the most diligent people I've ever known in terms of keeping in touch with family. They put consistent effort into making their nieces and nephews feel special and cared about with regular handmade birthday cards, detailed letters typed on a typewriter as they never owned a computer and thoughtful gifts. They were both retired high school art teachers and regularly sent presents showing off their artistic skills, like handmade jewelry, weavings, and other handmade artsy things. My mom always supplied a rude comment about how ugly or lame the gifts were, but I appreciated them. It felt so thoughtful that these people who rarely got to see me face to face went to the trouble of sending me a birthday card and a handmade gift to make me feel special.

The one thing I wasn't looking forward to about my brother's wedding was that my mom's sister, my Aunt Sarah, would also be at the wedding. I had intended to find a spare moment at the wedding to apologize to my Aunt Sarah for what had happened at Christmas. I still felt justified in my actions the prior Christmas and that our decision was the right one. But I wanted to apologize to her for how she had gotten caught in the middle of a situation that shouldn't have happened to begin with.

When the wedding day came, my Aunt Sarah glared at me and walked away from me any time I got near, and I didn't feel it was right to pursue trying to talk to her. The last thing I wanted was to cause a scene at the wedding. Instead, I had some pleasant chats with my Aunt Sophia and Uncle Ben. I did choose to speak up to my mom when she repeatedly accosted my dad for not taking photos on his camera on the wedding day. My dad had said he just wanted to be present and get to enjoy the experience of watching his son get married without having to be behind a camera. Plus, my brother hired a professional photographer, so there would certainly be no lack of good-quality photos. But my mom wouldn't let it go and continued to harp on my dad to take photos.

I defended my dad to my mom and said, "He's just trying to enjoy the day and be present."

My mom defaulted to her passive-aggressive tendencies by completely ignoring me the entire rest of the day, even when I complimented her on how she looked that day, she said nothing back to me. Passive-aggressive behavior often takes the form of backhanded compliments, avoidance of conflict, guilt trips, or feigning ignorance. These behaviors serve to convey hostility or signal resentment in a roundabout way. My mom was an expert in this behavior.

One particularly telling part of the wedding day that perfectly described the nature of my family was the wedding photos. It was time to take a photo with our side of the family and the photographer wanted a photo of just my parents, my brother, and me.

We stood next to each other awkwardly and the photographer tried a few poses, asking us, "Are you a hugging sort of family?", to which we all unanimously answered, "No."

That was an understatement. There was a blatant lack of closeness and affection in our family. Standing somewhat closely next to each other was the best the photographer was going to get, unfortunately, at a shot of a photo of a close family.

Shortly after the wedding, in early October, Gavin had his first performance with our church's children's choir. I made an effort to regularly invite my parents to Gavin's sports and school activities because I wanted Gavin to feel he had family support and presence at his activities. It wasn't uncommon though for my mom to initially make some random excuse for why she couldn't come.

She would say, "I can't make it because that's the night I do laundry."

She had always been exceptionally rigid with her home routines. She always did laundry on Wednesdays. Always. It was an entire evening affair where she meticulously separated every color from the others, held up every piece of clothing examining it for stains, and hung most of the laundry to dry rather than using our dryer. It was bizarre to me that she would be content missing her grandson's activities in lieu of doing laundry, which could be done any other day of the week. Unfortunately, my dad had to work the day of the choir performance, but my mom surprisingly agreed to come. When I said hello to her after she arrived, she ignored me and looked the other way. One of my friends at church came up to me and said hello and I introduced her to my mom.

My friend said, "Nice to meet you," to my mom, and my mom ignored her too.

I snagged a front-row seat inside our church sanctuary in my excitement to watch Gavin sing. My mom sat down two chairs to the right of me instead of sitting next to me, and our new church pastor came over and introduced herself to my mom. My mom obliged in shaking our pastor's hand but then gave her a stone-cold look and blew her off. I sat there stewing that she would be so overtly rude to people who were very important to me and to whom I greatly respected. After I got to proudly beam while Gavin sang his song with the choir, we all walked out into the church narthex area where everyone congregated after the service.

My mom tersely said, "Well, I'm going to go," turned around and just left.

No goodbye, no affectionate words to Gavin about doing well in his first choir performance, no thanks to us for inviting her. She just walked away. Passive-aggressive to the very definition of the word. Even Gavin remarked, asking why grandma had left so quickly. I made up some sort of excuse that she had something she had to get to. I honestly wasn't sure how to share the honest truth with my son that this was just the way grandma is.

But the reality is that inside I was beyond FED UP. I was so tired of her acting like a child. I was so tired of how she did not value or respect other people's feelings. I was tired of getting the silent treatment from her. I was tired of feeling like our entire relationship was one of obligation. I had no joy in seeing her. I loved her in a "you're my mom so I'm supposed to love you" sort of way. But the honest truth was, I had no emotional bond with my mother. I was always on guard around her, trying to protect my feelings and the feelings of my son and husband. I was very protective of Gavin, acknowledging that he was getting older and more aptly aware of how other people acted and treated others. The last thing I wanted was for my mother to begin to affect Gavin negatively the way she affected me.

It had taken far too long, but I had finally mustered the courage to face the issues with my mother head-on. This was a make-it-or-break-it point for me.

15

Everything You Say Can and Will Be Used Against You

It was at this time that I began talking to Tom about how I had been pondering going back to therapy to work on the relationship with my mother. He knew all too intimately the struggles emotionally I had been through because of her. I voiced to Tom that I would love to be able to heal that strained relationship, or at the very least, find a way to coexist without always feeling hurt and uncomfortable each time I saw her.

Being a therapist myself by this point, I carefully researched therapists to try to find someone I felt could relate to this family-of-origin issue I was having with my mother as I felt over my head. I found a therapist named Delia and nervously went to my first therapy session. As I sat in the waiting room for my first appointment to begin, I felt like all my feelings were bottling up in my throat. Delia put me at ease though. She sat in her chair with a cup of tea, a clear grace and calm emanating from her, likely from her prior time as a professional ballerina before becoming a therapist. I tearfully shared in that first session how I wanted to have a better relationship with my mother and detailed what the last year had been like. We also started to touch on what the relationship with my mother had been like while I was growing up.

From there, I met with Delia weekly, and, together, we quickly uncovered and put a label on the experience I had with my mother. Delia recognized many narcissistic tendencies in my mother and discussed the possibility that my mother may have something called Narcissistic Personality Disorder. Together, we talked about what this means. People with Narcissistic Personality Disorder have an exaggerated sense of self-importance, feel entitled, and need constant, excessive admiration. Narcissistic people exaggerate their achievements and expect to be recognized as superior. They expect unquestioning compliance with their expectations and will take advantage of others to get what they want. Additionally, they have an inability or unwillingness to recognize the feelings or needs of others. Not only that, they are often envious of others but believe others envy them, and will regularly behave arrogantly, coming across as conceited or boastful.

As a rule, even though I was a therapist, I resisted the urge to try to diagnose mental health issues in my family or friends. It wasn't my place. It was easy to wonder, though, if my mom could actually have this diagnosis. I'd be lying if I hadn't pondered over the years what may be at the root of my mom's behavior. I had told Delia of my own hypotheses. Was her inability to make friends due to a fundamental lack of social skills? Was it social anxiety? Was her pessimism about everything related to depression? Did she fall somewhere on the Autism spectrum? Did that explain why she had no awareness of others' feelings and didn't reciprocate in relationships? But plainly, none of these explanations completely fit nor explained the wide range of concerning anti-social behaviors she demonstrated.

As Delia walked me through the possibility that narcissism was at the root of what was going on with my mom, a light bulb clicked in my head. Delia was describing my mother to a T. Being a natural optimist, I had tried to overlook or alternatively explain these tendencies of my mother. But truthfully, these were always the characteristics that bothered and embarrassed me about her. How she would brag about herself in front of a group in a socially tactless way. How she would put others down or complain about others in a way to make herself seem superior. How she was consistently unwilling or unable to recognize or value my own feelings. How she always expected that I would just follow along with whatever she said no questions asked. How she made justifications and pointed blame at me or others and never admitted fault with herself.

During the first few weeks that I had been going to therapy with Delia, my mom emailed me asking me when they could babysit Gavin again. Tom and I agreed that we did not want her babysitting Gavin until we could work on improving the communication and relationship overall with my mom. We simply told my mom that we didn't need a babysitter at this time. Was what odd to both Tom and me, though, is that my mom didn't even ask to see us. She only wanted to see Gavin. She could have invited us over to her house or to meet up at a park together, but as soon as she heard we didn't need her babysitting, she dropped the desire to see any of us. I certainly got the unsaid message. Tom and I weren't important to her, just Gavin.

This was trademark narcissistic behavior. Narcissists often engage in triangulation in the family dynamic, where, in this case, my mother was trying to single out and separate my son from others in the family so my son could supply my mother with the admiration she needed and knew she wasn't getting from me. Narcissists may accomplish this goal by buying the child, or in this case, my child's love, by offering treats their parents don't normally allow, lying or manipulating the child into believing the fault lies with their parent or ignoring rules and limits set by the parent. Sound familiar? This is exactly what I had seen my mother do time and time again. Now that I no longer had blinders limiting my understanding of my mother's aims, I was able to prevent falling into the same traps I had fallen into previously.

I was able to open up to Delia about so many of the prior emotional hurts I had experienced at the hands of my mother. How I had tried in my teenage years to resolve issues with my mother and had written her letters to try to address my concerns. I discussed how those letters had felt useless as my mother would respond with sling-shot precision in placing the blame back on me and never taking responsibility for her own part in our conflicts. I had talked about whenever I would try to talk face to face to my mom about my feelings, I would clam up and end up getting choked up with tears, with my mind going blank, causing me to struggle to adequately express myself in person with my mother. I feared that even as an adult, I would end up having this same emotional flooding happen if I tried to directly address things face to face with my mom.

Because of this, Delia and I came up with a plan that I would write my mom an email detailing my concerns and hopes for a resolution. I knew that in my teenage years, letters hadn't proved fruitful in resolving issues with my mom, but this felt like my best option at this point. I carefully crafted an email to my mom, had Tom read it, and read it to Delia prior to sending it to my mom. They all agreed that the email was well thought out, detailed in a non-blaming way, and invited a more open dialogue. Not only that, but through talking with Delia about my mother's personality, we thought it would be worthwhile to call out at the beginning of the letter an acknowledgment that my mom may struggle in discussing emotions. Our goal was to try to validate how hard it may be to hear what I had to say and to try to disarm her from her common defense strategy of deflecting blame. In the email, I explained my feelings and how I was hurt because each time I had seen my mother since the Christmas incident, I felt like she was giving me the cold shoulder, and barely spoke to me. I told her that I wanted to get our issues out in the open in hopes of resolving them so that we could interact in a healthy way. I held my breath after I sent the email:

Dear Mom,

I am writing this letter in an effort to improve communication and make our relationship smoother. First off, I want to level-set a few things. I know that it is not easy for you to talk about your feelings or be vulnerable. I know it is not easy for you to talk through conflicts to resolve them. I know that you have feelings and at times they have been hurt, for instance, last Christmas. I can understand how that was a difficult day/experience for you. I know that you tend to get defensive, and this letter may trigger those feelings in you. I encourage you to have an open mind and hear the underlying tone and purpose of this letter, which is to find a way for us to get along.

With that said, I feel that for the last ten months I have gotten the cold shoulder from you, which has continued to hurt my feelings. I do not feel it is fair to be punished for the mutual misunderstanding that occurred last Christmas, and it has gone on long enough. I feel that each time I see you, you give me a cold grimace, do not say any sort of friendly hello, and the conversation between us is sparse, forced, and negative. When we part ways after gatherings, you barely acknowledge me, rarely say a nice goodbye, I love you, or much of anything else. If there is something else that we need to discuss to try to move past that incident, I am happy to do so. But I want you to know that if you continue to treat me the way you have treated me over the last ten months, I will not initiate additional get-togethers as I have dreaded our interactions over these last several months. Gavin has also started to pick up that Grandma treats me differently than she treats him or other people. If a young child is already noticing this, then it needs to be resolved.

I understand that you have a different way of communicating with others, and commonly much of what you choose to communicate in general conversation are things that have made you frustrated. I know that this is how you and your siblings communicate with one another and that seems to work for you in those relationships. I can understand how situations that make you feel frustrated are challenging and how you may be more inclined to talk about those things, as they may be fresher in your mind. From my perspective, however, I feel like the majority of what I'm hearing from you are those negative experiences, and often times it comes off to me as a stream of complaints. I would like to be able to empathize with you, but when the majority of what I hear is negative, it makes me feel in a worse mood and makes me want to withdraw and not pay as much attention to your conversation. I work very diligently to have a positive perspective on life. In my job I hear on a daily basis about people so depressed, that they have attempted suicide, have been victims of homicide attempts, or abuse, or are in the middle of some other terrible tragedy. Because of the nature of my job, I need to focus on positives for some balance. From my point of view, a waitress that didn't give you the greatest service isn't really worth wasting time complaining about. I am going to request that you attempt to limit the number of complaints and negativity you bring to the conversation when we do speak together.

You have continued to hint at wanting to babysit Gavin again and I want to take a moment to speak about this. There are multiple reasons we haven't requested your help babysitting recently. The first is a direct result of the poor and sparse communication between the two of us. When you have babysat in the past, I have asked for regular detailed updates on how Gavin is doing, and the majority of the time, I get a one-word answer that he's "fine" or something of the like. It has felt like too much work to try to get this communication rectified and I am left feeling in the dark as to how my child is, which is simply not comfortable for me as his mother. He is also getting to an age where he needs someone who can play and be really active with him, which is something that a babysitter closer to his age is better able to do. I am in no way saying that I do not want you to continue to have a strong relationship with Gavin as that is certainly not the case.

I want to be clear that I'm not expecting things that I do not think are possible. I know that we can find a way to better communicate and get along when we see each other. I feel it important to have expressed my feelings and what I need from you. I realize this may not have been an easy thing to read. I hope that you will take time to reflect on this and, again, understand the underlying hope that I have in writing this letter to you.

Love, Jackie

I got a response back a few days later from my mom and was not too surprised by the tone of her email. She was incredibly hostile and defensive throughout her email, bringing up issues from the past to justify her actions, and placing all of the blame on me. She clearly had no intention of trying to resolve our impasse in her email. She deflected what I had said by pointing the finger back at me. It was childish and hurtful. She launched into a few common defense mechanisms of someone with narcissistic tendencies, which most commonly include denial, distortion including exaggeration or minimization, projection or blaming others and enlisting the help of someone else who will support their distorted view.

Her email read:

Dear Jackie:

As you noted in your letter that it may be hard to read what you are writing without feeling irritated, this letter may also trigger those feelings in you as well.

I do love you and would like nothing more than to have a normal mother/daughter relationship.

Yes, I have feelings like everyone else, and those feelings were crushed when you rejected having a member of my family participate in a holiday that I haven't had any member of my family spend with me for over 30 years. My parents taught me that family comes first, no matter who they are, and you always make room for them. You note that it may not be easy to talk through conflict, but when I tried to reason with you on that day, you would not listen nor bend to anything I had to say. My feelings on that day were no different than what Dad felt when we lived in Pennsylvania and Sophia and Ben would not spend the Christmas holiday with us, but rather went to their friends' house as they usually do. He has not had a family member for Christmas either in as many years as I, if not longer, so he understood how I felt. When Tom's parents moved to Hawaii right after Andy graduated and left him with no one to spend the holiday with and he came to Minnesota, we were thrilled that he wouldn't be alone and would be with family.

If you feel that I don't initiate a conversation most of the time, it is because the times that I have you make me feel belittled. If I make a suggestion for anything, you say that it isn't what you would do or use or have, just flatly refuse anything I might have to say. Also, conversations won't always be cheery, sometimes they are negative, people just tend to discuss things that may have happened in their day, both negative and positive. I realize that you may hear that a lot during work, but that also goes beyond the workday as most people just naturally discuss those things with people they know. I don't think I have had any friend or coworker who hasn't bent my ear a time or two to vent something and they appreciate it. Sometimes you have to let people get it out and move on.

If you feel you need someone younger babysitting Gavin that is your choice, however, it is just for a couple of hours normally and we don't think that he would be hurt by having his grandparents do it so they can spend more time with him. We can do most things with him in an hour or so before he goes to bed that a younger sitter probably can, but as I stated, that is your choice. But we have also asked several times to have him stay overnight so we can spend more time alone with him, and never get the chance. As for how he is doing when you get home, we don't normally have a problem with him but if we do, we always say something, otherwise, he is a good kid to be with. The times we spend with Gavin are very precious to us.

Love, Mom

There were many things that stood out to me in my mom's letter. My mom also referenced having friends and coworkers to who she talks to. Again, I had never witnessed or heard about my mother having a friend. Also, my mom regularly complained and bad-mouthed all of her coworkers and told me how she sat by herself at lunch at work every day while she read books. I am not sure who she was referring to, but it only left me wondering who she was talking about or whether she had made that part up in an effort to make herself look better.

Again, in her letter, she mentioned how she wanted to have Gavin stay at their house overnight to spend time ALONE with him. Why alone? That made me suspicious and uncomfortable. It's almost as if she wanted to have me out of the way when she interacted with my son. Very odd. Yet again it is fitting with a narcissist's tactic of triangulating family members.

My mom also referenced in her email an issue that I had heard plenty of times through the years. She talked about how when my family had briefly lived in Pennsylvania when I was four and my brother was a baby, my Aunt Sophia and Uncle Ben had spent Christmas with their long-time friends instead of my family. But I know that these friends of Aunt Sophia and Uncle Ben were like their family, and they have literally spent every Christmas with them for over forty years. This was their tradition. My parents were apparently affronted that they would choose to spend the holiday with their friends instead of their family. But again, what was always lacking when I heard this story was my mother trying to understand my aunt and uncle's perspective. When later as an adult I asked my parents if they had ever told my aunt and uncle that they were hurt by this incident, they said no, they had never brought it up. This was also so typical of them. Instead of addressing an issue head-on, and trying to resolve it, they passive-aggressively bad-mouthed my aunt and uncle behind their backs. They held on to their resentment and their own perspective alone, rather than recognizing both sides of the situation. My mom's use of bringing up this past event served to pit me as the one in the "wrong" as they had always pitted my Aunt Sophia and Uncle Ben.

I processed this emailed response from my mom with Tom and with Delia. Tom wasn't at all surprised by the reply my mom had sent. From everything I had shared with Delia, she wasn't too surprised either. When someone who behaves narcissistically is challenged, they resort to these types of defense mechanisms. Delia did encourage me to consider how I can begin to better protect my feelings if my mom wasn't willing to work on these issues. Delia encouraged me to begin to assert myself more directly in communication with my mom. If my mom wasn't willing to make any efforts to improve communication or relations between the two of us, I was going to need to spell out specifically what I needed and expected. I needed to set some boundaries to protect my own emotions. I needed to be bold and clear. My follow up email to my mom read:

Dear Mom,

I received your letter. I will also let you know that I have been seeing a therapist myself to get some help working through this issue as my feelings have continued to be hurt. My therapist encouraged me to write a letter to you. She also warned me that I may get the type of response that I received from you and I wish I could say I am surprised that she was right. Not once in your reply did you attempt empathy for my feelings and instead continued, as you have my entire life, to invalidate my feelings and make me appear to be in the wrong. It is astonishing to me to witness a woman such as yourself who has never in my entire life admitted any fault in how your own behavior may negatively impact someone else. The way you've treated me has led me to withdraw from you. It also led to me, at age 19, almost attempting suicide and ending up in the hospital where a social worker had to confront you that you couldn't even so much as hug me as I sat in the hospital shaking and sobbing. It is just pitiful that you continue to treat me this way. I do not deserve it.

I am expecting no miracles here that your behavior may change. But I will be putting up much stronger boundaries with you from now on. I will not be initiating any get-togethers with you. If I am around you and you begin to rant and complain as I have clearly in my prior letter asked you not to do, I will walk away from you immediately. I never ask for "suggestions" as you call them from you as I don't want them. You volunteer your suggestions in a condescending manner so you can make yourself seem like your way is always best. I don't need it. If that continues, I will also be walking away from you.

Do not ask to have Gavin stay at your house any longer as that will not be happening. You've made it clear in your reply that you have no intention of providing me with meaningful updates on how my child is doing when I'm not there, which is not to make sure you're fine in handling him but is instead to make sure he is thriving himself, and therefore your babysitting will no longer be needed.

My mom did not respond to my email and instead sent a very random email to me asking about phone plans. She didn't reference my last email sent to her at all.

After further conversation with Delia about how triggering my mom's emailed responses, or lack of responses, were to me, we made the mutual decision that it would be best that I send my mom one last email asking her not to email me anymore. I told her that I was taking a break in my communication with her and if something urgent came up, to call Tom instead. I couldn't bear the thought of receiving another defensive email blaming me for everything. Tom had graciously agreed to act as a mediator between me and my mom regarding any needed communications for the time being.

16

Better an Oops Than a What-If

After the email exchanges with my mother, Delia suggested that trying to resolve things directly with my mother may be fruitless. Knowing that my mother had some obvious deficits in being able to recognize or understand other people's feelings meant that it was unlikely that she would be willing to try to recognize my feelings in a way that would be needed in order to have healthy communication. I shared with Delia that my dad would at times try to be the peacemaker and was the one parental figure that I felt had at least some willingness to recognize and respect my feelings. As such, Delia suggested that I instead try to communicate with my dad and ask him if he'd be willing to act as a middleman in helping to repair the relationship with my mother. Delia hypothesized that to some degree, my dad likely recognized that my mother had deficits in understanding feelings and being able to resolve conflicts, likely resulting in his pattern over the years of stepping in to comfort me when my mom wouldn't or couldn't. I hoped that since my dad cared about both me and my mom, he would be able to assist us in the repairs needed in our relationship. I had no intention of pitting my dad against my mom so tread very carefully in how I would broach this idea to my dad.

From there, I emailed my dad asking if he would be willing to act as an intermediary between me and my mom to help us resolve our conflicts. He replied that he was willing to do so. He also told me that he had some further thoughts about my mom's and my recent email correspondence that he wanted to share and sent me the following email:

Dear Jackie,

Yes, I have read mom's response and yes, I have seen hurt feelings from both of you. This has weighed heavily on me for some time and actually made me physically sick. Things happen in all relationships and there are ups and downs. We all love each other and that is all that really matters. It is <u>now</u> time to move on from whatever happened in the past and enjoy each other with the time we have left. I don't want to see this go on another day. Please do this, I know mom wants it badly.

Love, Dad

I will be honest that my initial inclination after reading my dad's email was to seek clarification about his reference to becoming "physically sick." It made me wonder if there was some sort of larger medical issue that he was dealing with from this stress. I admit I am naturally a more anxious person. I had carried a deep-seated level of anxiety since childhood of an underlying fear that my dad wouldn't be forthcoming in sharing his medical issues with me as he got older. Only a few years prior he had told me much after the fact that he had gone to the hospital thinking he was having a heart attack only to find it was a hiatal hernia. He had smoked cigarettes for about thirty years before finally quitting when I was a teenager, and I had a pervasive worry about how deeply that had affected his health. My dad also made frequent laissez-faire remarks about how he didn't care to get regular medical check-ups or physicals. He didn't exercise and ate terribly. His favorite snack food was Twinkies. To be frank, I was also afraid that of my parents, my dad would die first, leaving me alone with my mom as my only remaining parent. I couldn't even imagine the dreadful family dynamics without my dad as a safety net. So, I wrote him back:

I appreciate your reply. To ensure I am understanding your communication correctly, could you please clarify what you mean by physically sick? I will respond more fully to the rest of the letter when I am more prepared to do so.

My dad sent back a one-sentence response:

It made my stomach upset.

His response eased my fears at least. But I realized that I was dealing with a rapidly increasing amount of anxiety after I started the ball rolling in broaching this larger relationship issue with my parents. I felt like I had opened a can of worms I knew was going to explode but didn't know how it would eventually resolve itself. Throughout all of the email correspondence thus far, I continued to meet with Delia and process the communications with my parents. She remarked on how my dad was very quick to reference just putting things behind us and getting along as if we could just brush the past under a rug and pretend it never happened. Together, Delia and I also decided that trying to communicate through email wasn't proving productive. It was very triggering to me as I would have to wait days for a reply and my anxiety was extremely high with the worry of the type of response I may get. Delia suggested instead that I try to plan some phone calls with my dad.

Again, I expressed my concerns about how my dad could monopolize conversations and my emotional overwhelm would often result in me starting to cry, getting frazzled, and not being able to properly express what I had hoped to talk about. As a result, I had to be planful. I went into phone calls with my dad by preparing and writing an outline of the points I'd hoped to cover. Tom also provided me a lot of reassurance that he was available to me for comfort if things took a turn for the worst on the phone call.

Unfortunately, phone calls with my dad quickly proved to be counterproductive. He consistently fell back on his suggestion that we just needed to "move on" and "get along." He didn't understand that this wasn't immediately possible. I couldn't just snap my fingers, and everything would be better. He didn't understand that I couldn't just hop back into a relationship with my mother destined to repeat old unhealthy, hurtful patterns. It had taken a great amount of courage for me to finally open up about the years of hurt and pain I was holding on to. After I had vulnerably thrown out all of that and been so transparent with my feelings, only to have them ignored and berated, did not lend itself to being able to move on. I felt even more invalidated by my dad's reactions. Emotional invalidation occurs when a person's thoughts and feelings are rejected, ignored, or judged. It's a terribly painful place to be caught in.

My dad would also throw out excuses saying that my mom "hasn't always had the easiest life, you know," so I should give her some grace.

I didn't know what he was eluding to and he didn't elaborate beyond telling me that he worked a lot when I was young, and my mom was alone in caring for two kids. I tried empathizing and validating that, but again tried to reiterate my point that even despite that, it was not an excuse for the emotional neglect I endured and that I couldn't just pretend it didn't happen. I found myself dissolving into tears during phone calls with my dad, him berating me and guilt-tripping me at how negatively this was impacting him and my mom, with no expression of empathy at how this was impacting me negatively as well. I had many mixed feelings at the reaction of my dad. I had expected more from him, to be honest. I had always known that he tended to be quick to anger, but at the end of the day, he had been at least moderately reasonable and empathetic as I grew up. The fact that he was so strongly defending my mother without an ounce of willingness to see that there were some concerns present surprised and baffled me. At the time I didn't recognize the very likely potential that if my dad defended me even a little, that he could be putting a wedge in his relationship with my mom or risk her turning against him. Ultimately because of this, he couldn't stay neutral or try to see both sides.

In trying to make sense of this situation I was caught in, my mind wandered back to a Psychology lab class I took during my undergraduate education at Luther College. We were paired up with a lab partner and given a rat my partner and I affectionately named Rizzo. Rizzo had a large cage that included wood shavings for a bed, a water bottle the rat could drink from, and a metal lever affixed to the wall of the cage. Our task was to teach our rat that in order to be given water, it had to press the metal lever with its little paw. Through behavioral strategies, we were successful in teaching our rat the association between pressing the lever and the reward of the water.

In a twist of fate, we also had to observe and document the rat's response if the water bottle reward was taken away. While our initial prediction was that the rat would quickly learn that pressing the metal lever was no longer fruitful given it no longer got the water reward it had become accustomed to, we were surprised to learn a very different outcome from our rat. Once the water reward was taken away, the rat didn't give up pressing the lever. Instead, it doubled down its efforts and began pressing the metal lever wildly, over and over again, almost incredulous that it wasn't working to give the desired water reward anymore. It took a significant amount of time for our rat, Rizzo, to eventually abandon her efforts at pressing the lever for the water.

In many ways, my dad was now acting quite a lot like Rizzo the rat. He was used to me being quite easily manipulated into compliance and following the status quo as he prescribed it. When he wasn't getting the expected outcome from me of giving up, he doubled down in his efforts and layered on his tactics even more heavily, hoping to get the desired outcome once again he hoped for. But I knew I had to persevere if I wanted to teach my dad that these old methods weren't going to work anymore.

As the weeks and months drew on, I continued to try to work on this relationship with my mom, and ultimately also with my dad. But I had a tremendous spike in anxiety throughout the day and night. Nighttime was the worst, though. I would lay awake for hours, my mind just racing and replaying all these emails and phone calls that just served to beat me down emotionally. When I finally fell asleep, I would wake up early in the morning once again repeatedly reliving these feelings again. Each night I would lie in bed and just cry and cry, trying to let out the feelings of hurt I was experiencing at once again being told that my feelings weren't real and didn't matter.

In many ways, I was mourning the childhood I had had and the recognition that I didn't get what I needed emotionally growing up. As Brené Brown said in her book *Braving the Wilderness*, "Not belonging in our families is still one of the most dangerous hurts. That's because it has the power to break our heart, our spirit, and our self-worth." I literally wept for that little girl who wasn't comforted or cared for the way she needed. The girl who didn't belong or fit in with her family. The girl who was too sensitive. The girl who had always felt like she wasn't liked or wanted by her mother. Tom, being the wonderful man that he is, would hold me and comfort me each night through my tears. He was my rock and beyond patient throughout this ordeal. I legitimately don't know how I would have gotten through this whole process without the support of Tom by my side.

I have always loved to read, and early in our marriage Tom and I had together read the book, *The Five Love Languages*, by Gary Chapman. As part of the book, there is a quiz that helps you determine what your top "Love Languages" are, in terms of how you appreciate receiving love. What stood out to me in going through this book is that my top two love languages were "Quality Time" and "Physical Affection". Receiving that feedback from the book served as further validation for me. Here it was, a clear outline of what I needed in order to feel love. I needed meaningful bonding time together and physical comfort and affection. No wonder I had grown up feeling like an empty well, so unloved, and uncared for by my mother.

Delia and I discussed that what might be helpful at this point was to write my dad a letter, and then get together with him face to face, and read the letter to him directly. This would allow me to fully express my feelings without getting so frazzled when just speaking off the cuff and inevitably forgetting the point I was trying to make. It would also allow us to be able to have some back-and-forth conversation about my letter immediately afterward. So, I asked my dad to meet me for coffee. Again, I prepped the letter I would share with my dad, had Tom read it, and Delia. We all agreed that the points I made were important, that I expressed my feelings appropriately, and moved towards finding better boundaries in the relationship with my mother. I didn't sugarcoat things. I needed to be brutally honest and specific.

Sitting together with my dad in the private room at the coffee shop, I read the letter:

Dear Dad,

There are some things I need to share with you. The information I am going to share with you is going to be hard for you to hear. It may hurt your feelings. Please understand that this is not the intent of the letter. The intent is for me to be honest about my feelings so I can be crystal clear that you now know what my personal experience has been. If you react with yelling, belittling of my feelings, defensiveness, and excuses for actions taken, I will not listen to this and will walk away.

I am sharing this information with you individually apart from Mom as I do feel that you have a capacity for empathy and a capacity to show you care. Additionally, if this was an issue just between you and me only, I feel there would be a hope of finding a resolution. Unfortunately, I have no hope that Mom has the capacity to resolve this conflict. I am hoping that you will be able to reason with her in a way I am unable to. I know that this situation between us has been very difficult for you as well. This situation is much larger than just the incident that occurred last Christmas. It is also not a situation that one can just move on from and forget.

Very importantly, I need to let you know that I have NEVER had my emotional needs met by Mom. Not in my entire life. My entire life, she has either ignored my emotions, made me feel bad for the way I have felt, or told me my emotions were wrong. I have consistently been emotionally invalidated. Because of this, I have suffered. I have been immensely hurt. I have dealt with periods of depression since the age of 14. I nearly attempted suicide at age 19. It is the reason I have distanced myself from her in adulthood. I have had to protect myself. Most recently I have been seeing a therapist myself to get help in working through how to live my life with the type of mother I have been given. I will not allow her to continue to negatively impact my emotional state any further. And even more importantly, I will not allow her to do the same to my son as she did to me.

I will not listen to any defensiveness around this subject. I do not care why she acted the way she has; I do not care what her rationale is for the way she has acted toward me. There is no excuse, there is no rationalizing it. It is not OK. She may think she's done right as my mother, but she is wrong. The biggest thing I have learned by becoming a mother myself is that being a mother is about being the kind of mother that your child needs, not the kind of mother you think you should be.

Mom has had a persistent inability to respect or understand how she can make someone else feel bad or worthless. I have even attempted to defend you with Mom when I have seen her walk all over your feelings at times too. Just recently at Charlie's wedding, I stood up to her when she ridiculed you in front of Sophia and Ben for not wanting to take the photos yourself during Charlie's wedding. She couldn't understand how you may have feelings that differed from hers. This has been my experience my whole life. Mom is incapable of understanding that others have different opinions and feelings than hers and that it is not acceptable to assume that her opinions are the correct ones and to undermine others when they have different feelings or are hurt by her actions.

Moving forward there are going to be drastic changes to my relationship with Mom. These changes are not negotiable. These changes have been put into place to protect me and my mental and emotional health.

Moving forward this is what you can expect from me:

- *I will no longer be seeing or speaking to Mom moving forward. I will not visit your home. This is the way I can best protect myself.*
- *I will not be allowing any babysitting of Gavin in the future. He will not be spending the night at your home. I am not comfortable with this.*
- *We will not be spending holidays all together any longer. You are more than welcome to see Gavin, but it will need to be on the day before or after the holiday, for instance, and I will not be present. Instead, Tom will be there with Gavin.*
- *I am happy to visit with you apart from Mom. I respect if you decline this, but I want to let you know that I would be happy to do this.*
- *If you would like to see Gavin with Mom present, you can come to my home or a public area. Tom will be present, and I will not be there. If Mom does not respect the below expectations for her behavior, Tom and Gavin will leave.*

The following are expectations I have for how Mom interacts with my family. If she refuses to respect these requests, then she will not be seeing Gavin any longer. Expectations:

- *I will not allow Mom to laugh when Gavin is sad or hurt. I will not allow her to undermine any feelings he expresses. Examples of undermining his feelings are saying that he's just sad because he's tired, wants attention, etc. He is allowed to feel exactly how he feels.*

- *Complaining will not be tolerated. Legitimate serious personal issues are welcome to be shared. A conversation about positive highlights of your lives is a welcomed conversation topic.*
- *When Mom interacts with my family, she will greet them with a polite hello and a smile. If she gives a cold grimace that will not be tolerated.*
- *We will no longer accept unrequested goods from your home. We have repeatedly asked mom not to give us things from your home that she doesn't want. We expect this wish to be respected.*
- *We will not allow any unrequested suggestions. If a direct question is asked of Mom, her suggestion/response is welcomed. Providing her suggestions for things that were not asked of her is unwanted and will not be tolerated.*
- *Tom and I will not be undermined as Gavin's parents. We are his parents and our way, and our say goes.*
- *There will be no yelling allowed toward me, my child, or my husband.*
- *We will not allow presents to be given to Gavin outside of holidays such as Christmas, Easter, and his birthday. What he wants and needs is quality time spent with you, not presents, which only reinforces materialism, not love.*
- *We ask you to not bring him sugary treats except on Christmas, Easter, or Halloween. If you would like to bring him a food treat, other acceptable options include his favorites, such as grape tomatoes, or other healthy snacks.*

You do not have to agree with my feelings or the reasons for what I have outlined above. If Mom would like to continue to have a relationship with my son, this is what I require of Mom. If she is unwilling to do these things, then that relationship will be over.

You may be wondering if I am suggesting that I will never see Mom again. I can't provide an answer to that right now. I can say that based on the 33 years of behavior I have experienced with Mom, if that same behavior continues, then my relationship with her will be over. The only current possibility I can imagine that may change my feelings would be, for instance, if she sought her own therapy with a therapist who can help her work on appropriate ways to express empathy to her daughter, and how to validate other people's emotions. As I have outlined above, without consistent evidence of change in her behavior towards me, I have no desire to continue a relationship. This is by no means an easy decision for me to make. However, it is time for me to find the courage to stand up for myself and how I deserve to be treated. It is for the sake of my own mental health because I need to be able to surround myself with people who build me up, rather than tear me down.

I am also happy to speak further about anything I have outlined above. If I can help in providing clarification, I am happy to do so. I will not listen to any rationalization for Mom's behavior, however. Thank you for taking the time to meet with me.

Love, Jackie

When I finished the letter, my dad looked furious and the first words out of his mouth were, "That's not my wife."

I responded calmly, yet tearily, by saying, "Well, that's my mom."

At this, he abruptly stood up and began to walk out of the room. I tried to stop him by asking if we could talk more and he said that he would be in touch and just walked out. I dissolved into tears. I felt abandoned. I had put my heart on my sleeve in sharing so many emotionally laden details of my past with him. And his only response to me was the invalidation of my experience. Complete denial. I let my tears run dry, composed myself, and went home. Tom was waiting to hear how it had gone and hugged me in comfort at not getting the reaction I had hoped for. Even with this hurt, though, I still felt proud of myself for speaking my truth. Because that's exactly what I did. That WAS my mom. That was MY experience with my mom. I never eluded that she was a terrible human being or a terrible wife to my dad. I tried very hard to speak from my own experience. I continued to tell myself that what I had said needed to be said and ultimately, I was glad that I had the courage to do it.

Though my letter to my dad may have come across as harsh, the firm boundaries I outlined in my letter were an absolute necessity. I set the boundary right off the bat in my letter that if my feelings were belittled as I read through my letter, I would not stay there and would get myself out of the situation to protect myself from further hurt. Boundaries are an interesting dynamic in that they don't serve to directly alter the other person's behavior, in this case, my dad's, but instead, make it clear that if they engage in certain behavior, my own response will be different from what they are used to. In this case, if my dad launched into his common behavior of rationalization, then I would not just sit and endure it like he was used to. The end result and goal of setting a boundary is to change the power dynamic and bring more control to my own circle, where I can decide what I will and will not tolerate.

17

The Squeaky Wheel Gets the Grease

I waited on pins and needles for weeks to hear from my dad as he said he would be in contact with me. But there was no communication despite what he had promised. Finally, I could wait no longer. I was honestly scared to talk to him on the phone for fear that my mom would inadvertently answer if I called, so I defaulted to sending him an email:

Dear Dad,

I want to let you know that I have been trying to be as patient as possible, but I am very angry and frustrated at the lack of communication on your behalf.

Our last conversation was nearly two months ago, at which time you told me that you would be getting back to me. I realize that you are likely still processing through all of the different things that we have discussed, but you have not held up your end of the agreement which was that you would be getting back to me. If you hope to move forward, it is going to take effort on both of our behalf. Thus far, I feel as though I have been the only person who has taken the initiative to express my feelings and offer ideas to make things work better.

I would appreciate knowing what you intend to do to try to help in resolving this issue in our family dynamics. If you are not interested or willing to try to resolve these concerns any longer, please do me the decency of letting me know. That will allow me to move on with my life. Finally, I ask that you no longer email me anymore in the future. To assist with more direct and healthy communication, please call me directly on the phone and I would also be happy to meet face-to-face as well.

Love, Jackie

Wouldn't you know it, but my dad EMAILED me back:

Dear Jackie,

Yes, I am emailing you, and you will just have to deal with that.

Sorry you are angry, just as I was after we last met. I will give you a call in the next couple of weeks after I discuss more with our counselor. But when I do call, I do expect positive steps on your part to end this. I will not accept condescending tones or words or any attempt to demonize mom. And yes, this situation has dominated mom and my thoughts daily. I know I do not have that many years left, and this must end.

Love, Dad

A great many thoughts and feelings flooded me after receiving this email. Certainly, anger dominated initially, feeling that my dad had very intentionally and condescendingly opened his email by throwing it in my face that he was emailing me despite my having asked him to more directly communicate. Clearly, the dynamic between me and my parents had escalated to becoming a battle. Secondly, I was surprised at seeing a reference to the fact that my parents were seeing a therapist. He hadn't mentioned this to me before, but I felt like this was at least a positive step in the right direction. Third, I felt annoyed that he was trying to put me in my place by stating that he was not going to accept condescending tones from me or attempts to demonize my mom. This was just blatantly out of the left field and felt like he was talking to me like I was a little kid instead of another adult. I had been extremely intentional in my communications with my dad to remain calm, respectful, and stick to the facts and feelings of the situation. It was also clear that he had no ability to recognize that I wasn't trying to paint my mother as a monster, but that on the contrary, I was trying to explain how things she had done over the years had negatively affected me.

My dad's reference in his email to not having many years left seemed like a slimy form of manipulation. That somehow because he was now in his sixties, that meant he was almost on his death bed so I should just forget everything and put it behind me. What a cop-out. The only alluding to empathy in his entire email was the short "sorry you're angry," which really wasn't empathy at all. It felt like the kind of apology a kid who's not really sorry gives when his parents make him apologize, where he just blurts out a quick, "sorry," and moves on.

I continued to apprise Delia as to this most recent communication from my dad. She also remarked on how my dad was defending my mother completely with no room for admitting that there may be even an ounce of fault on her behalf. Delia pondered whether there was some level of codependency between my parents. Codependency is an excessive emotional or physical reliance on a partner, typically one who needs support due to some sort of deficit, illness, or addiction. This could explain my dad not being able to psychologically tolerate any potential negative feedback about my mother, his insistence on defending her, and his inability to even consider that my experience as my mother's daughter could be different from his experience as my mother's husband. This was the nuance that ultimately bothered me the most. I was not saying that my mom was a horrible person or that there was something wrong with their marriage. If they were happy together, that was wonderful. If things between them worked well, that was great. But the fact of the matter was that my experience was different. My experience as a daughter was unique in my family system. With my dad being a man, he may just not have been able to understand what a daughter may need from a mother as that can be very different from what a son needs from a mother or what a son needs from a father. The fact that he couldn't even begin to consider that my experience was real and valid hurt more than anything.

It was around this time that Delia asked if I thought my brother had any idea what was going on between me and my parents. I told her that I honestly had no idea. I hadn't spoken to my brother in several months since his wedding, which wasn't altogether unusual for us. Delia and I discussed why it would be helpful for me to talk to him. As a member of our family, it was important that he know why there was tension in the dynamics at this time. It was also important for him to hear from me, that I had no inclination whatsoever to have him forced into picking sides, that he didn't have to agree with my perspective, but that I wanted to ensure there was healthy communication with him about what was going on. So, I called my brother and left him a voicemail asking him to call me back. He didn't. This wasn't completely unusual for my brother, who was notoriously flaky with getting back in touch with people. I called him again and left a more detailed voicemail about the reason I was calling. Still nothing. Then I texted him. No response. Then I emailed him. Nada. I was becoming suspicious that maybe my parents had gotten to my brother first and perhaps this was the reason he wasn't calling me back.

My dad did not keep his word to call me back as he had said in his last email, despite me waiting several additional weeks to hear from him. I had been sitting with my now ever-present annoying friend, anxiety, this whole time. Once again, I bravely initiated a phone call to him and tried to start it off on a positive note, saying that I thought it seemed like a helpful step that they were seeing a therapist. My dad didn't open up much about it, only to say that they found it helpful and had only had a couple of sessions so far.

Then he launched into an abrupt dialogue about how his therapist had said of me, that, "If you are a Christian, shouldn't you be able to forgive Mom?"

I thought to myself, "Forgiveness? What exactly was there to forgive at this point?"

There had not been any true acknowledging or addressing of the core issues, nor even any remote semblance towards resolving these issues. How could we jump ahead ten steps to forgiveness already? And to throw my being a Christian into the same sentence as if to say that I was a hypocrite and not following my own faith principles?

I responded to my dad by saying, "In order for there to be forgiveness, there needs to be an apology and resolution of the issues first."

I went on to say that I had not heard one word about how my mom intended to change things between us. The only thing I had heard from her was her complete denial of the issues, blame towards me for there being issues, to begin with, and absolutely no willingness on her behalf to acknowledge my concerns or change anything. I asked my dad point blank if my mom had expressed any willingness to work on changing how she treats me and Gavin.

My dad responded back with the blandest of replies, "I think so."

I THINK SO??

He may have just said, "Not a chance," because that's what I heard between the lines.

My dad tried wrapping up our conversation like so many of the prior ones by saying that we need to just put this all behind us and move on. Again, slapping a band-aid on a situation that could not be ignored any longer.

Before the call ended, I asked my dad if they had talked to my brother about what was going on between us. My dad said yes, that they had let my brother read the letters and emails I had sent. I was stunned. Those pieces of correspondence were not meant for my brother. Yes, I wanted my brother to know that there were problems in our relationship but had hoped to be able to have a dialogue about it, rather than just have him read one side of the story. I told my dad that I was hurt that he would share my letters directly with my brother. I told my dad that I tried to get in contact with my brother but that he wasn't returning my calls or emails.

My dad said, "Well he's not happy with what you did."

I asked if my dad had encouraged my brother to talk to me about it. He said no. This didn't surprise me at all. This felt backhanded and manipulative. My parents weren't encouraging my brother to try to hear both sides of the story. They had clearly made this move in an attempt to sway him to their side. Talk about being hypocrites. For all the sludge they had dragged me through about not allowing my Aunt Sarah to come over to my house, and how we were "supposed to be there for family no matter what." And now they seemed to have no problem with my brother not speaking to me. They had made no efforts to try to keep him impartial. I was just dumbfounded and didn't have much else to say at that point, so the conversation ended quickly thereafter. My dad said he would call again soon.

As you may have guessed, I waited more weeks with no phone calls from my dad. I had initiated this revision in the relationship with my parents but still fell into the trap of not recognizing how old patterns were destined to repeat themselves. Being strung along with no feedback from him was very painful for me. I felt like I had been left in the dark and duped. I finally called him again and asked why he hadn't called me back yet. He made a dismal excuse about being busy with work. I didn't buy it but let it go.

My dad suddenly blurted out, "I'm sorry that you were suicidal in the past."

I could tell that he was trying to be brave in bringing up this pertinent message that I had shared in my letter with him at the coffee shop. It was at least some form of empathetic response that I was grateful for.

My dad went on to tell me that he thought he should tell me that his own dad had committed suicide.

I quickly said, "Oh my gosh, I'm so sorry. I never knew that."

The story I had heard was that my paternal grandfather died two months before I was born of prostate cancer that had eventually spread into his bones. My dad went on to tell me that his dad had been in tremendous physical pain from cancer and that he understood why he took his own life. I responded that I was still really sorry and that he must understand to a degree the type of suffering a person must be in to consider suicide. I was hoping by saying this that it would help him understand that the pain I had been through that was worsened further by the issues with my mom had led to my own thoughts of suicide. But my dad's level of denial was too strong to let this sink in.

My dad said, "Jackie, I was there. I saw your relationship with Mom, and it was not like that."

This statement from my dad was a calculated tactic called countering, which is part of the arsenal of tools someone uses in gaslighting another person. Countering occurs when someone attempts to manipulate another person by questioning or denying the memory of an event. My dad said that he saw my mom as loving and caring. I told him that I was glad he felt that my mom was loving and caring, but that she was not this way to me. I added that yes, he was there when I was growing up, but he certainly was not there for every single minute and moment. I also said that it was very possible for two people to have drastically different experiences during the same event. I told him this was not a reflection of how he was towards me. I told him that a mother-daughter relationship is different and there were certain things that I really needed from a mom that I didn't get. He just couldn't let this information in. He went on to say that my mom even bragged to her coworkers about me. Hold the phone. What? I had never heard a single positive piece of feedback from my mom in my entire life. All I could make of this was that my dad was grasping at straws to find some excuse to show that my mom ultimately did care about me. And the truth was, it wasn't that I didn't think on some level that my mom cared about me. I tried to believe that she did. But the reality is that I never ever received the KIND OF love and care I needed. She wasn't able to meet my emotional needs in the WAY that I needed.

I processed this jarring phone call with Delia in another therapy session. Delia pointed out that my dad's response to my past suicidal thoughts was somewhat curious. Delia thought the phrasing of how he said he was "sorry that I was suicidal" was kind of a cop-out.

It was like saying, "I'm sorry your feelings got hurt," instead of the very different, "I'm sorry what I said hurt your feelings."

The latter at least show some acknowledgment of how what they had done had affected me. It was an important nuance. There was no acknowledgment in my dad's statement recognizing that my mom played a role in how I felt alone and ultimately suicidal. There was no acknowledgment from my dad in realizing that he was aloof as to how I had been suffering at that time.

Not only that, but Delia heavily praised me for how I stuck up for myself when my dad tried to cut down my experience by telling me that he had been there too, insinuating that I was making things up or misinterpreting the truth. I was allowed to own my experience. My experience was real. Delia encouraged me to trust my gut and trust my own truth in my experience. This wasn't easy for me. My dad continued to try to manipulate me by inserting self-doubt in me and I resented that. He was really embodying the term "gaslighting." I knew what I was saying was the truth. It had taken me thirty years for goodness sakes to be able to say it out loud to him. I knew that I had not jumped into this lightly. This was very important to me and I wasn't going to let my experience be undermined.

Finally, Delia found the part of the conversation with my dad where he threw out that my mom bragged to her coworkers about me to just be more validation of my mom's narcissistic tendencies. Delia hypothesized that my mom likely was using me as a tool to make herself seem grand by association by pointing out my achievements to her coworkers. Clearly, the goal of my mom sharing about me with her coworkers was to pump up her own ego. It certainly wasn't for my benefit.

It was around this time that I had finished reading a book that Delia had recommended to me called, *The Emotionally Absent Mother: How to Recognize and Heal the Invisible Effects of Childhood Emotional Neglect,* by Jasmin Lee Cori. This book was life-changing for me. It literally felt like I was reading my own autobiography. Every single page of this book validated the lifetime of hurts I had accumulated from my emotionally absent mother. There were many stories that were so closely reminiscent of my own experiences with my mother that it was startling.

Part of why it had taken me until my early thirties to finally address these matters directly with my mother, is that I had long struggled with this inner tension about the issue. On the one hand, I felt lucky that I had grown up in a middle-class home where at the end of the day, I always had enough to eat, clothes, and even many luxuries that others often don't experience. Many people had life experiences much worse than mine. I wasn't physically or sexually abused. Basically, all of the hurt I had felt over the years was invisible. I had struggled to give merit to my own experience because of the guilt that others were worse off than me, so why should I complain? But reading Cori's book helped me put a name to the neglect that I had very much experienced emotionally. I didn't have to compare my pain to others. I didn't have to feel guilt at admitting that my struggles were real. I didn't have to worry about what others would think. But these messages were challenging to accept.

By not having a nurturing mother capable of attending to my emotions, I had grown up with this pervasive sense of being not good enough. I had long struggled with having low self-esteem and often lacked the self-confidence to do things because of this nagging self-doubt. I never felt that my achievements were good enough. I didn't like the way I looked and always felt overweight even when I wasn't. In social situations with new people, I often held back for fear of being embarrassed or coming across as unintelligent with nothing to say. The experience with my mother profoundly affected me. Was it all her fault? No. Of course not. Our lifetimes are a compilation of a million different experiences and interactions with others. Our own temperament and innate nature play a huge role too. But what happens when you are born a naturally more emotionally sensitive person and then you have a mother who is completely incapable of validating and tending to that? You end up getting hurt. You end up feeling like something is wrong with YOU. And that is how I felt. Alice Miller nails this concept in her book, *The Drama of the Gifted Child,* that "far too many of us had to learn as children to hide our own feelings, needs, and memories skillfully to meet our parents' expectations and win their "love"."

I can never begin to fully express how much I healed through my therapy experience with Delia. She helped me by providing the emotional validation I had long been searching for.

She straight-up said the words to me that I had always been afraid to say out loud: "Your mom was not the kind of mom you needed."

And it was true. She wasn't. She wasn't able to be. I don't ultimately know why. But I did know that I was tired of continuing to open myself up to repeated hurt from her. I had to take action.

Late in May, it was my birthday. I shared with Delia how I had always dreaded seeing my mom on my birthday. Into adulthood for my birthdays over the last few years, I had intentionally planned to get together with my parents the day before or after my birthday so my actual birthday day would not be spoiled. I had experienced way too many years of uncomfortable interactions with my mom on my birthday. She wouldn't ask me how I was, asked me nothing about myself, gave me a gift that was in no way personable, and would sit and complain and suck the joy out of the room. Given the strain in the relationship with my parents at this point, I had no idea if my parents would even acknowledge my birthday. My birthday came and I got a card in the mail from my parents' return address. I intentionally waited until the day after my birthday to open it as I didn't want to be triggered on my actual birthday. It was a nice card but when I opened it, it was only signed by my dad.

This was incredibly uncharacteristic. Both my parents always signed the card. I would have hoped on some level that my mom would have signed the card in acknowledgment of some sort of care for me. But again, I was still stuck in the idea that my mom was capable of more than she was showing. Her lack of message or signature spoke loud and clear.

18

A Ruffled Mind Makes a Restless Pillow

Delia, being a marriage and family therapist, walked me through a few options for how we could move forward. She asked if I would feel comfortable having a joint family therapy session where we would invite both my parents to join me and Delia. We talked through this option and it made me really uncomfortable. I could imagine my mom sitting there with a frown on her face the whole time, sharing one-word answers, pointing blame at me, and my dad jumping to her defense. I did not imagine this scenario being a productive use of time.

As an alternative, Delia asked if I would be open to doing a family session with just me and my dad instead. I said that I thought this could be more constructive and that it would help to have Delia there for support in case I ended up feeling flustered and losing my train of thought, which happened so often to me when interacting with my parents. Delia suggested that it could help to first have a session with just my dad and Delia alone. This way, Delia could break down my dad's potential defensiveness at coming to therapy with the therapist he knew was already working with me and had a therapeutic alliance with. She said that in that session, she intended to act as more of a neutral body to help reinforce how I wanted to work towards a resolution of the issues, but that we needed to do the work to resolve them first before we could just move on and put them behind us. Delia also suggested that she could also start to get a gauge of whether my dad was willing to do this work at all, which could help us be more informed about whether pursuing conjoint therapy sessions with me and my dad together would be fruitful and productive. I agreed that this plan sounded helpful.

Delia also helped me be prepared for the possibility that instead, my dad might suggest that we alternatively have a conjoint session with my parents' therapist instead. We discussed how this was not going to be beneficial. Given the level of denial already voiced by my dad and the complete unwillingness of my mom to admit to the issues at hand, it was highly unlikely that their therapist had any sort of true, accurate picture of the core issues going on. Furthermore, we also felt suspect as to the style of their therapist given my dad sharing how his therapist had thought I should be able to forgive mom if I was actually a Christian. This had rubbed both Delia and me the wrong way and didn't feel it likely that their therapist would be able to facilitate a helpful conversation with my family.

I ended up calling my dad and posing the idea of him having a therapy session with my therapist. I shared what Delia and I had discussed that this could be an opportunity for him to hear a bit more of my experience from my therapist's perspective and that from there, we could potentially have a session together. He agreed to have the session which slightly surprised me but made me hopeful at the same time.

Delia and I planned a therapy session for the two of us together the day after the session she was going to have alone with my dad so we could process how it went. I was a ball of nerves waiting to hear how it had gone. When I sat down for my session with Delia, she quickly told me that overall, her session with my dad went well and that my dad shared more than she had anticipated he would. Delia explained how she had helped reinforce the fact that two people in a family system can have very different experiences and feelings than one another, even though they lived in the same house. Delia also shared with my dad how I felt on eggshells around my mom and that I could never truly be myself. She told my dad by way of an example of this, how I had even long suspected that my mom had been married before but never had the courage to ask outright if that was true.

Delia shocked me by telling me that my dad had replied, "Yes, we were both married before."

What?!?! My jaw hit the floor. I told Delia that I had never known that my dad had also been married before. Delia apologized as she thought I would have known that information with how casually my dad brought it up to her, a complete stranger. Delia had thought I just hadn't ever known if my mom had been married before. Delia went on to share that she had processed with my dad a bit more about my mom and their marital relationship. Apparently both my parents had been married before they married each other, and their prior partners had both had infidelity concerns prior to their divorces. Delia said my dad had hinted that my mom's first husband may have been abusive as well. This was certainly all news to me! Could this be why my dad was so defensive in protecting my mother's image and denying my experience? Was he afraid of having another failed marriage so was willing to do whatever it took to keep this one untarnished? Was my mom's passivity in reacting to my dad's history of impulsive anger reactions because of her own history of domestic violence? I was left with a great many more questions and fewer answers.

Delia also said it struck her that when she had asked my dad what qualities had initially drawn him to my mom that my dad had said, "She was cute."

Delia and I both thought this seemed incredibly bland and immature. It's something a junior high kid would say about a girl he liked. Not something we expected a grown man to say about the wife he'd been married to for over 30 years.

She would have expected him to say something like, "She was caring, smart, funny, a great friend..."

But no. He said she was cute. That was it. When Delia pressed my dad a bit more as to other qualities of my mom that he admired he said that she was a great cook and a good companion. Certainly, I could read into this response all day long, but ultimately, whatever works for them in their relationship is fine. I'm very glad if they are happy together and all is well in their relationship. But the reality is that my dad really couldn't identify any positive traits to my mom's personality. It seemed like what kept him in the marriage was companionship. Was this what I needed in a mother though? No. Not by a long shot. Delia helped me process through the shock of hearing all of this new information, especially the long-kept secrets about my parents being married before. I told her how unsettling it was not only to know that my parents had kept this from me my entire life but to find out in this manner.

I also revealed to Delia an incident that recently happened at my church. Very coincidentally, there was an older married couple, the Charleston's, at church that had known my parents when they were first together and newly married, back before I was born. They had originally been friends with my dad and then knew my mom once they were married. This family had moved around a lot just as my parents had, and it was a completely random happenstance to find out that both of our families had landed back in Minnesota. They had lost touch with my parents after all those years, but I thought it was kind of neat to meet someone who had known my parents even longer than I had. Occasionally, this couple from church would politely and jovially ask Tom or me how my parents were when we would see them at church. One day they were talking with Tom after the church service, asking how my parents were. Tom had told them that there was a strain in the relationship, and we hadn't seen them recently.

The husband of the couple said, "Oh, is it related to Sean's [my dad's] drinking problem?

I know that used to be a big issue." Tom was pretty stunned as he and I were none the wiser in knowing that my dad had had some sort of problem with alcohol in the past. Tom reassured them that that wasn't the issue, and respectfully, didn't share any details about what the strain was about, to honor everyone's privacy.

Tom told me after church what he had found out. I shared with Tom that I should be shocked but wasn't. After finding out the secret that had been kept about my parents' first marriages, who knew what other secrets they were keeping from me. Certainly, they have the right to their secrets, but secrets generally lead to feelings of distrust.

For self-care, I was still consistent in seeing Delia weekly for therapy sessions throughout this entire process with my parents. I shared with her about finding out my dad had had a problem with alcohol in the past. Delia pointed out how my parents likely had a lot of shame about these secrets they had held onto for so long. I could certainly understand that. I understood why you would be ashamed to share with your daughter these sorts of things.

Even with all that continued to transpire throughout this time, I still felt like I wanted to move forward with having a conjoint therapy session with myself, my dad, and Delia. I hadn't let go of the hope that we could find better ways to communicate. When it was the day of our session, my dad and I walked into Delia's office. My dad was stiff but friendly. Delia and I had prepped for this session and decided that she would introduce what our goal was, in terms of wanting to improve communication and help my dad understand why this issue was so important to me. She also planned to turn over the conversation to me after her intro, so I would have a chance to express my feelings to my dad without him beginning to dominate the conversation or swing the topic in a different direction. Delia also overtly encouraged my dad not to leave the session suddenly, and instead, if he became angry or overwhelmed, we could take a break and rejoin when ready. Delia said this to my dad to protect my feelings and to hopefully avoid ending up in a similar circumstance as the prior coffee shop meeting I had where my dad deserted me after I opened up to him.

I tearfully shared with my dad that what was at the root of the issue with my relationship with my mom was not getting my emotional needs met growing up, and how into adulthood, this had negatively impacted my self-esteem and my ability to feel open and comfortable around her. I also shared how I was starting to see this same pattern emerging with her interactions with Gavin and that it was my job to protect my son and ensure that he wasn't negatively affected by her. I restated that I hoped we could figure out a family dynamic that resulted in the least amount of emotional pain.

My dad relaunched back to his default script of, "I just never saw this. This isn't how it was."

Delia jumped in for me and reinforced that this was my experience, regardless of what he saw from his perspective. Delia was attempting to thwart my dad's continued efforts to gaslight, or deny, my experience. Unfortunately, the remainder of our session together was much the same. My dad continued to reject any of my personal experiences. But I was proud of myself because instead of getting so distraught and feeling rejected, I held strong to my experience. I knew that what I was saying was MY TRUTH.

My dad said that he and my mom were going to counseling together and when Delia probed a bit at what they felt they were gleaning from their therapy experience, he said, "Learning how to talk more about feelings."

When Delia asked if my mom was able to recognize any part that she had played in the issues with me, my dad glossed over it and said, "Somewhat."

This did not instill in me any form of hope that my mom was, in fact, open to admitting any personal responsibility. The rest of the therapy session was filled with several bizarre comments from my dad that didn't seem to make sense.

One of these comments occurred when Delia asked how this situation had impacted my dad, and he said, "We've lost friends because of it."

When Delia and I asked him what he meant, he said that the couple, the Charleston's, aforementioned from our church who they had known years ago were no longer talking to them. I was very confused because I had no idea how that related to me at all. From what I knew, my dad was lucky if he talked to this couple once every five to ten years at the most. I certainly never said anything to the couple from church about the specific issues with my parents. Tom had only shared a tiny snippet of there being a strain in the relationship. That was it. My dad clarified that they knew that my best friend's parents, the Weston's, who happened to be in a faith group with the Charleston's, had told them all about what was going on and had pitted them against my parents. I couldn't believe he would make such an accusation. Yes, I had talked to my best friend about this and also to her mother, who at the time was one of the pastors at my church. But I knew that both of them held that information in strict confidence. There was absolutely no way that they would ever say something to this couple from church, much less try to pit them against my parents. I told my dad just this.

My dad continued to restate that he felt like we just needed to move on as he "didn't have that many years left."

This again felt like a manipulative guilt trip to me, and I responded that no one knows how much time they have left. That didn't change that there was going to need to be work done to move forward. We wrapped up the session by asking my dad if he would be willing to have more therapy sessions together potentially. He cautiously agreed. It seemed as though he thought that this one session that he had come to today should have been sufficient.

The oddest part of the session was literally as my dad was walking out of the room, he asked me in front of Delia, "Hey, could Gavin come over to our house for a few hours this weekend?"

I was completely blind-sided. I fumbled initially and paused before I blurted out, "Um Dad, were you just here?" In my head, I thought, "How would you think we're ready for that step?" I told him, "No. We have a lot we still need to resolve before I would let Gavin come over to your house again." He seemed shocked and then simply walked out of the room and left.

Delia and I had planned that she and I would have a half-hour session just the two of us after the session with my dad so we could process what had transpired.

After my dad left, Delia and I both stared at each other dumbfounded and I said, "What was that?!"

How could my dad think we could just jump from our session where literally nothing had changed and there had been not a sliver of resolution, to ask if we could go back to normal and have Gavin come hang out at their house? Delia agreed that she was really surprised at his gusto in asking an obviously ill-timed question.

In processing with Delia, we both agreed that it seemed like my dad's mindset in coming to this session was that he was going to show up, check the box of attendance and that everything would go back to normal afterward. Likely in his thought process, he left the session thinking we would just put everything that had happened behind us, and that is why he asked such a pointed, poorly thought-out question. I told Delia that this session just reinforced that it was clear that neither of my parents was making forward strides in trying to understand my feelings. My dad couldn't say even one thing that would be different moving forward.

19

Let Me Be Me, or Let Me Be

In further therapy sessions, I shared with Delia that I felt like I needed to make a decision. I needed to decide whether I felt like it was even worthwhile to seek a resolution with my mother and whether I could continue a relationship with her at all. Delia helped to normalize the fact that some adult children do choose not to have a relationship with their mother, and that this was an option for me. It was not one I had honestly ever considered before this. I felt like I had this imaginary ball and chain tying me to my mother that would be there for eternity. I certainly did not jump at this option, but it felt somewhat liberating to know that this option was even on the table. Delia also guided me as to other options. She shared that another choice could be not having a relationship with my mother, but still having one with my father if he was willing. I thought this through but could see quite vividly how this would play out. I could see my dad continuing with insistence each time I saw him that I put the past behind me with my mom, trying to guilt-trip me and that there would be a constant tension between us.

What I was really searching for was peace. I wanted to be able to feel comfortable in my own skin. I wanted to be able to live my life authentically. What this meant to me was being able to be myself. Being myself meant that I could stand up for what I believed in, and communicate to others in a caring, assertive manner. I could have feelings and express them. I wanted reciprocation in my relationships. Of course, in life, conflicts and disagreements arise all the time. But I wanted to be able to address those conflicts head-on. I felt able to do this in every other relationship in my life except with my parents. I had gone out on a ledge in opening up to both of my parents about my feelings. I had taken a chance. I had been very vulnerable in sharing what I felt deep down. Did I expect them to be able to digest years and years' worth of information from me in just a second? No. I certainly could understand on one hand how what I was sharing could come across as a shock to my parents. But it had literally been almost a year since I had started the process of opening up to them about my experience. I thought I had given them ample time to at least take a tiny step towards acknowledging my feelings. And still, nothing had changed. I was certainly caught in an impasse.

I felt exceedingly angry and exhausted. I was tired of being strung along. My dad hadn't been able to give me any sort of clear idea of what sort of progress they were making in therapy and how that would positively impact our relationship. I knew that I needed to make a change. I needed a much stronger boundary. I needed to have some sort of closure. I spent a lot of time praying and talking to Tom about what I should do. I weighed the pros and cons of each of the possibilities. I ended up considering four separate options.

The first option was that I could continue to just wait around with the smallest sliver of hope that my mom would change. I could wait and see if we could ever find a healthy way to coexist and interact together without continued emotional pain. I could open myself up to what would likely be months if not years of family therapy with my parents to try to improve our relationship. Being honest with myself, though, I knew that the likelihood of my parents agreeing to participate in family therapy for the length of time required to make real improvements were slim. Even slimmer was the potential of my parents, especially my mom, having the openness to hearing me out and the willingness to make changes that therapy ultimately requires in order for improvements to happen.

The second possibility I considered was that I could just have a relationship with my dad and not my mom. I knew that with this option, there would always be this hurt hanging over my head, and that he also didn't believe my experience. There would likely be ongoing resentment by my dad that I wasn't interacting at all with my mom. As I had seen in the prior months, too, I could imagine a constant message from him urging me to put the past behind me and just move on. I didn't want to deal with that ongoing constant pressure to just forget what happened knowing that history would most certainly repeat itself.

The third option I thought of was that I could build a boundary with both of my parents and no longer have a relationship with either of them. This way, I could acknowledge that the relationship with them was causing me unyielding emotional harm and needed to end. But I felt internally guilty about even considering this, because of how much societal pressure I felt telling me that I was supposed to have a relationship with my parents no matter what.

Lastly, I considered just continuing to have a relationship with both of my parents, knowing that nothing had changed in the relationship dynamic. I could choose to consciously limit the frequency that I saw them to just a couple of times a year. But here's the thing. I knew that this would be a very challenging and slippery slope. Would we invite them to Gavin's birthday celebrations? What if they continued to put pressure on us to see Gavin more often? What if each time we saw them they tried to make us feel guilty for not seeing them more often, or put us on the spot in front of Gavin asking if he could come to their house? I could definitely imagine that each of these scenarios would be highly likely. I could also see that each future interaction with my parents would be even more forced and artificial, with their denial of my experience hanging over our heads. I did not have confidence that my parents would respect boundaries as they had so clearly overlooked them in past experiences.

Certainly, none of these options were ideal. What would have been ideal would have been my parents having even the slimmest of open minds when hearing about my experience. What would have been ideal is for them to show some empathy for how this situation had affected me over the years. Then I would have felt more comfortable and confident in continuing to have a relationship with them. This would at least show me that there was some hope of change for the better.

Delia really aided in opening my eyes to the wide variety of relationships people have with their parents. She shared that she's had plenty of clients over the years who have had varying levels of relationships with their parents. Everything from only seeing their parents once a year, to only having a relationship with one parent, to not having a relationship at all. I worried that if I no longer had a relationship with my parents, Gavin would feel like it was his fault somehow. That was the last thing I wanted.

I let all this stew for several more months. As much as I wanted to make a decision and have some sort of peace with whatever decision I made, I didn't want to make a decision hastily. During this time, it was radio silence from my parents. They made no attempts to contact me. This only deepened my sadness. I felt sad for my parents for the anguish that they were dealing themselves from what I had shared. I still wondered if they felt any empathy at all for me and the emotional distress that I had been under through all this? Their pervasive silence only caused me to feel more unsettled. As my parents, I felt like the least I could hope for was even a check-in call asking how I was or if I was coping alright with everything. I didn't receive that. Then again, I was thinking about what I would do as a parent in that case, not what they would do.

I reflected almost obsessively about what I should do. I really tried to consider how each of the potential paths I could choose made me feel. This required a lot of honest mindfulness work. Mindfulness has become a buzzword in therapy, but anyone can engage in mindfulness. The practice of mindfulness involves creating a mental state where you focus your awareness on the present moment, calmly accepting your feelings, thoughts, and bodily sensations. For me, I had to pick up on my own internal queues as I thought through all of the various possibilities before me. This was really a groundbreaking time for me. Being able to decide for me what was right. To not have to worry about all the potential ramifications, but instead to trust myself and honor my truth.

That's not to say I didn't worry, though. I constantly had a push and pull battle between being honest with myself and anxiety about what was the right thing to do. I struggled with terrible nightmares every night for months and months. A common theme of my nightmares involved my parents abducting Gavin. What I gleaned from this theme of my nightmares was that I really was afraid of how all of this would end up impacting Gavin. In my heart, I didn't believe that my parents would ever do something blatantly harmful to Gavin like abducting him. But I did still have some irrational fears about it. My mind clearly was wandering when I slept to those very scary possibilities.

When I reflected on it all, I knew in my heart that the only path I could ever be comfortable with was a clear-cut one. I needed to be able to feel peace and freedom. I needed to not feel the weight and burden of holding onto a relationship that continued to hurt me. Especially knowing that literally, nothing had changed in that relationship. And from everything I had heard, neither of my parents had voiced any sort of willingness to hear out my perspective or honor my wishes by making changes to the relationship.

After a great, great deal of thought and reflection, I knew in my heart that the best decision for me was not to have a relationship any longer with either of my parents. When I imagined what life would be like with this decision, I found that feeling of peace and freedom I had been yearning for. Deep down in my heart, I knew that this was the right path.

I also knew that it was going to be anything but easy. I knew that I was going to have to consider how best to clearly communicate this to my parents. I would need to talk to Gavin about what this all meant and why it was happening. I would also need to share this information with friends and family. This was going to be no small task. It would also take a lot of emotional courage on my part to be brave enough to take this step.

With Tom and Delia's help and support, I drafted a letter that I would send to my parents letting them know my decision to end the relationship with them. I sent the letter through certified mail as I wanted to make absolutely sure that they received it. Once I had sent the letter, I felt free. I felt a tremendous weight lifted off my shoulders. I knew that it was the right decision for me. The letter to my parents read:

Dear Mom and Dad,

This is the last letter I will be writing to you. This letter is to say goodbye. I will no longer have a relationship with either of you moving forward. Gavin will also no longer have a relationship with either of you moving forward as well.

Much has gone into this decision. In the last year, I have been working as hard as possible to avoid this outcome but none of my efforts have been fruitful in getting through to either of you. I have held onto emotional pain throughout my life caused by Mom and now worsened by the recent actions by Dad. When I wrote the first letter to Mom almost two years ago, I expressed hope of resolving conflict and finding a way to co-exist without my experiencing continued emotional pain. What I received from Mom was a typical response expected from her-spiteful, deflecting, refusing to take responsibility for her actions or to change.

Following this, I tried to work with Dad in an effort once again, to try to resolve the conflict by using Dad as a mediator between my and Mom's relationship. Dad, I do appreciate that you were at least willing to try to help. What I experienced from Dad, though, was cold and uncaring emotional abandonment and an inability to even provide a basic acknowledgment of the experience that I did have growing up with my mother. Mom, your silence these last many months has spoken louder than words.

The worst part of this last year for me is that I have spent so many sleepless nights worrying about hurting both of your feelings and making every effort I could, to be honest in a respectful, clear, direct way, and what instead has become all too apparent is that neither of you has an ability to acknowledge or respect my feelings. What I have been yearning for since beginning this journey of trying to resolve things with the both of you is to hear even the most basic caring and compassionate acknowledgment of my experience such as, "Jackie, we are sorry for not giving you what you needed in terms of emotional support in your growing up years. We will make every effort we can to change that moving forward because we care about you." I have come to realize that expecting to hear something like this is nothing but false hope, as even through these last two years, more than enough time to come to terms with what the issue is, you have yet to give me empathy or compassion. You also have given me no information about what you intend to do to change moving forward to correct the way that things have been. I have no desire to willingly continue in a relationship that I know is destined to provide me with ongoing emotional pain.

Because I have no hope of either of you changing, I will not knowingly have my son continue in a relationship that has the extremely strong potential of emulating the experience I have had. I have attempted to ask for a change in how you interact with my son, but you have disrespected and disputed each of these attempts. I care deeply for the emotional health of my son and will not allow him as he continues to grow, to further realize that he is helpless in the way he's treated by the both of you and make him feel as I have felt: disregarded and uncared for.

This situation is particularly sad because as much as you cite things like "you do anything for family," those are just words and not backed by any honorable actions. You demonstrated this in how you inappropriately involved Charlie in this situation by intentionally attempting to sway his opinion to be on your side. I do hope to have a relationship with Charlie moving forward, but because of the damage that you caused, it is yet to be seen if that is possible.

I do appreciate that you have gone to therapy, but I have seen no change that you have shown as a result. I do hope moving forward that you seek additional help regarding the end of our relationship, but even if you do, that will not change this boundary in my and Gavin's relationships with you as we proceed ahead. In an effort to be as crystal clear as possible, when I say that Gavin and I will no longer be having a relationship with either of you, it means that I do not want any communication of any type from either of you in the future and we will not have any communication with either of you as well. This is not going to change regardless of a change in your or my health, or other circumstances in life. I am not going to change my mind and I am not proceeding with this lightly.

Lastly, I do not wish ill upon either of you. Whether you can believe this or not, I hope you are able to eventually find peace. That is exactly what I will be working towards as well. I know for myself that the only way to do that is to leave this negative relationship behind and be able to move forward with my life and put the hurt behind me.

Love, Jackie

20

The Kids Are Alright

After sending the letter, I knew that there were likely going to be people in my life that wouldn't understand or agree with my decision. If I had suffered physical abuse from my mom, others would never have second-guessed why I chose to no longer have a relationship with her. But emotional abuse and neglect are different. It can go unnoticed, indistinguishable to the naked eye. It's also subjective. Some may not understand emotional neglect as a sufficient reason to choose not to continue a relationship. There were likely to be others that may look down on me for severing ties with my own parents. But I held on to my own truth that this was the right decision for me and my family. No one else had lived my life or experienced exactly what I had. So ultimately, no one else had permission to place judgment on a decision that was based on my own unique experiences and feelings.

That didn't eliminate my own fears and worries about telling others about my decision. I tend to be a person who once I make a decision about something, I feel like I need to act on it immediately. Some of that boils down to my own anxiety management. For me, if I can get something over with, it is less anxiety-inducing than sitting around stewing about it and worrying about what could happen. Delia encouraged me to pace myself, though. I had already been through a lot and needed to tend to my emotions.

I also needed to mourn. In all reality, I realized that I had long ago mourned the loss of the relationship I had always wanted with my mom. As a teenager when I began to slowly accept that my mom was never going to be the kind of mother I needed, I started to grieve that loss. But the loss of my dad was not something I had ever anticipated. So that mourning needed to happen. And it did. I shed many tears and felt the tremendous heavy sadness that the loss of the relationship with my dad had been the side effect of this much bigger issue with my mom.

I also knew that I wanted and needed to let Gavin know of my decision to end the relationship with my parents. Months earlier, we had a conversation where Tom and I both sat Gavin down on our couch and I shared that he may have noticed that mommy had been sadder than usual and that I wanted him to know why. I shared in kid-friendly terms, that my parents, his grandparents, were not being kind to me or respecting my feelings. Because of this, I was seeing a counselor to get help with it. In my home, going to therapy is something we communicate as a strength, not a weakness. I also shared that it was my job as his mom to protect him. I wanted to make sure that my parents never ever treated Gavin the way they treated me. Gavin was incredibly understanding and in his own kid way, seemed to get it.

Tom and I again planned how we would communicate to Gavin that we were no longer going to have a relationship with my parents and what that also meant for Gavin. When I shared with Gavin this news, I was intentional about sharing it in a way appropriately suited for a child. I emphasized that he had done nothing wrong, that this was not his fault, and that my parents still loved him. But I was clear to share that it was our job as his parents to make sure we protect him and not allow people to be around him who don't treat him well or don't treat us well. I communicated with Gavin that our little family, Gavin, Tom, and me, will always look out for each other and will always be together. I emphasized that there will never be a time when we don't have a relationship with each other because we will always work through our problems together. This messaging was so key for me to communicate. Gavin received this news calmly and voiced his understanding. He continued to ask me questions about it for months to come, but I was very open in validating that it was normal to have questions and that I would be honest with him always.

When I expressed my relief at how well Gavin had received the news with

Delia, she commended me further. She shared that Gavin likely absorbed the news so well because he has a strong emotional attachment and bond with me and Tom and knows that we will care about him no matter what. That bond reassures him he will not be abandoned or mistreated and that we will always be there for him.

Additionally, Delia suggested what I had long suspected, which was that the relationship between Gavin and my parents was more superficial. Gavin never had a true emotional bond with my parents because their primary way of showing love was through gift-giving, which was more artificial. So many of my own worries about Gavin's reaction to my news were unfounded. This really cemented to me that I had built a very different relationship with my child than the one between me and my mother. Whereas I never felt like I could be open and put my feelings out there with my mother, my son knew that he could talk to me and I would respect his feelings no matter what. It brought such contentment hearing Delia's outside perspective of the relationship between Gavin and me, confirming how intentionally different it was from my own relationship with my mother. This is exactly what I had always wanted. This is exactly what I had worked so very hard to achieve. I felt immensely proud that I was able to break this cycle of emotional neglect with my own son.

From there, I updated my closest friends. I have a wonderful group of strong, smart, supportive women as friends, many of who had been friends since college. I had slowly opened up to my friends along the way about the struggles I was going through with my parents. I was relieved to find that my friends respectfully listened to my story and the subsequent reasons I chose to discontinue the relationship with my parents. They were ongoing supports to me in ways that I found truly touching and healing.

Being very involved in my church community, I felt it important to open up with my pastor about what had transpired with my parents. Tom had been on the hiring committee with my church to hire our newest pastor about a year prior. As such, Tom had gotten to know her well and had opened up a bit about the fact that I was going through a lot with my parents. My church was always so wonderfully supportive and encouraged families to let them know how they could pray for us. My pastor had checked in with me and said she would love to get together some time to talk and see how she could better support me. I felt so cared for by this action. I set up a meeting at the same coffee shop I had previously met with my dad at. It felt quite symbolic to me to reset that place and make it have a positive association rather than having a negative connotation associated with it. Pastor Annie was so gracious in how she listened to my story without judgment. She provided me affirmation and support for what I had gone through and how hard the decision was that I had faced regarding the future of my relationship with my parents.

In thinking of what family I may want or need to talk to about the state of the relationship with my parents, I knew that there was no one on my mom's side of the family that I felt comfortable reaching out to. I really wasn't close to any family members on my mom's side of the family nor did I feel like it was likely to be productive or helpful to talk to them. Alternatively, on my dad's side of the family, I had my Aunt Sophia and Uncle Ben. I also had my Aunt Shirley, my dad's brother's wife, who was still living, though my Uncle Todd had passed away a few years prior. I also had two cousins on my dad's side of the family, Katie, and Chris. I felt it was worthwhile to talk to them about this issue as they were in my life and I wanted to be as honest as possible. I also did not want what happened with my brother to repeat itself. I wanted to be able to share my side of the story with my family. But I was determined to communicate with my dad's side of the family in a respectful, neutral way, and hold fast to my message that I in no way wanted to tarnish the relationship that my extended family had with my parents. I only wanted for there to not be an elephant in the room regarding what was going on with the dynamics with my parents.

I sent the following letter to my Aunt Sophia and Uncle Ben:

Dear Sophia and Ben,

This isn't an easy letter to write but one I feel is important to send in order to help make you aware of the state of the relationship with my parents at this time.

I have been seeing a therapist for the last two years in an attempt to work through some very long-standing issues, primarily between my mother and me. I won't go extremely in-depth about this, but the gist of the conflict is the emotional neglect I've experienced from my mother since childhood. She has been a cold, distant, uncaring person toward me in the many milestone moments one needs a warm, compassionate mother. Into adulthood, this concerning dynamic negatively impacted me as my mother lacks healthy conflict resolution tools, and instead, when there have been conflicts or disagreements, I am shut out, given the cold shoulder, and blatantly ignored when I see my mother.

In the last year through my own therapy, I've come to terms with the effects this challenging relationship has had on my own mental health and have attempted to address this issue with my mother. I've worked with my therapist to share with my mother how the interactions between us have negatively impacted me and asked for our relationship to change in ways that will help us both be able to interact together without experiencing more hurt feelings. I have felt proud that I have been able to ask for these things in a kind, mature fashion. Unfortunately, my mother lacks the skills and the ability to accept what I have asked for as something that I deserve and has shut me out further.

Upon realizing this was the direction things were going between my mother and myself, I enlisted my dad to try to act as a mediator in helping us to work further on the family dynamics. I have spoken to my dad many times over the last two years and even attempted a couple of sessions with my dad and my therapist together to try to work on this issue further. Unfortunately, my dad directly refuted my experiences with my mother and demonstrated that he and my mother were unwilling to change. The biggest concern I was faced with was seeing how my mother had begun to emotionally manipulate my own son and started to treat him in ways she had towards me as a child. I simply cannot allow that to occur and am extremely protective of the emotional health of my son.

After a very long road of attempting to find a middle ground or some form of way to relate to each other that would not continue to cause emotional pain, it was evident that is simply not possible. As a result, and again with the guidance and encouragement of my therapist who I trust very deeply, I decided to sever ties with my parents at this time. My family (myself, Tom, and Gavin) won't be having contact with them moving forward. This was one of the hardest decisions I have had to make and not one I entered into lightly. I continue to pray for them and hope that at some time their hearts will become more open to acknowledge the pain I've experienced in the relationship with my mother and find a way to change. At this time, I'm not hopeful that this will occur.

I want to say emphatically that I am not sharing this information with you in an attempt to sway your viewpoints of my parents or alter your relationship with them in any way. That is definitely not what I want. I do recognize though, that in a family, openness and honesty are important and I didn't want you to find out about this situation offhandedly, and instead wanted you to hear it straight from me. I recognize you may have more questions than answers right now about what all this means, but what I would ask is that you continue on as you have in terms of being wonderful, kind family members who I know care deeply for those in our family. I continue to care for you as well as my parents, but sometimes boundaries are needed in order to protect us from further hurt. I do hope that you may be able to find some level of understanding regarding that. Thank you so much and much love to each of you.

Jackie

I then sent a very similar letter to my Aunt Shirley and my cousins Katie and Chris. I was nervous to hear the reactions of my family members but felt pleased in how I had worked to be very tactful in how I communicated what had gone on. I got responses back from everyone I had sent letters to. The responses overwhelmed me. Each of their responses was filled with compassion for what I had gone through. They shared that they knew this wasn't an easy decision but supported my decision, nonetheless. Each family member communicated that they cared for me deeply and would continue to be there for me in any way they could be moving forward. I was so immensely grateful for the graciousness and love they communicated to me. After so many months of being invalidated by my parents, this felt like a breath of fresh air.

I continued to see Delia for therapy to continue to process my feelings after all of this change and transition. I shared with Delia the feedback I had gotten from my extended family on my dad's side. Delia hypothesized that my extended family on some level, likely saw exactly what I was describing in my mother. Though we didn't get to see my extended family on my dad's side very often as they lived in Pennsylvania and Georgia, when we were all together, it was clear my mom didn't really fit in with the rest of the family. Delia proposed that likely my extended family could infer that what I shared about emotional neglect made sense from their own interactions with my mom.

Tom continued to be an invaluable support to me throughout everything I had gone through with my parents. He supported my decision to sever ties with my parents 100%. I could not be more grateful for the amazing man that Tom is. Together, Tom and I also discussed letting Tom's family know that we were no longer going to have a relationship with my parents. We knew that they may at some point ask about my parents and wanted to stave off an awkward spur-of-the-moment discussion.

Subsequently, a few months later, during a family gathering with Tom's middle brother and our sister-in-law, we sat around a campfire after Gavin had gone to bed for the night. Tom's brother checked in with me about how things were now that we had moved on from the relationship with my parents. I found that I was able to be really honest and authentic with them in sharing what had led up to the decision and why we had ultimately decided to no longer be in a relationship with them. My brother-in-law and sister-in-law were also very caring, and supportive throughout my sharing this information. They had had some interactions with my mom over the years at our wedding and birthday parties for Gavin, so had seen first-hand how off-putting my mom could be.

The reactions of our friends and family to my decision were far more positive than I could have ever predicted or imagined. I was so relieved that by and large everyone had been so understanding. No one had shamed me for severing ties with my parents. No one had tried to guilt-trip me or make me feel bad for what I had done. This confirmation was so refreshing.

21

Hold Your Breath

One of the lingering fears I had after building the permanent separation from my parents, was whether they would actually honor and respect this boundary. I worried that they would still try to get in touch with me in some manner. I wanted a clean break. I wanted to truly be able to move forward and let go of this emotionally laden baggage I had been carrying around with me.

Only a couple of months after I ended the relationship with my parents, I had an unfortunate accident while biking. I ended up breaking my leg and had to have surgery to repair it. I had posted something on Facebook about it, and my brother's wife, my sister-in-law, saw it and told my parents. While I was still in the hospital, Tom got an unexpected phone call from my dad. Tom didn't pick up the call and instead, my dad left a voicemail.

Tom told me the voicemail was contemptuous and that my dad said, "Call me and tell me what happened to Jackie. I'm her father and I have a right to know."

The remark Tom made was that it was an odd way of phrasing things.

Not, "I heard that Jackie got really injured and I'm worried so want to know what happened." Or, "Is Jackie OK? I just want to know that she will be alright."

Instead, it was a very territorial response. Like, he's my father so he has the right to know all that's going on with me. Tom was concerned that my dad might try to just show up at the hospital unannounced if Tom didn't respond.

So, Tom texted my dad and told him what happened but that I would be fine. We also took the precaution of asking the front desk not to allow visitors back without my approval. Being in a fragile state in the hospital where I couldn't walk made me feel very vulnerable. The last thing I wanted or needed at that time was to have a confrontation with either of my parents. Thankfully this fear was unfounded as they did not appear during my time in the hospital.

As of the writing of this book, that was the one and only attempt at contacting us that my parents have made. As time went on, I was able to relish in feeling relief that the boundary was being upheld.

22

Freedom is What You Do with What's Been Done to You

As days turned into weeks and weeks turned into months, time moved on. I continued to notice how much peace I felt about my decision. I felt relief. And calmer than I had literally been in years. I did not feel regret or guilt that I had made the wrong choice regarding the path to move forward with my parents. I continued to pray for my parents daily and hoped that they were finding support of their own in coping with the change in our relationship. But I ultimately knew that the boundary I had set with my parents was the right one. This way, I could continue to live my life without constant worry about the dynamics with my parents, but also be able to instead focus on the love that deep down I still had for them. This was an important reminder that I told myself. Even though I was no longer in an active relationship with my parents, it did not mean that I wished ill will upon them or stopped loving them. On the contrary, I still loved them and wished them peace as well. The old adage, "If you love someone, set them free," developed a new meaning. Despite still loving my parents, I knew that I couldn't let the relationship continue the way it was. I also couldn't trust or believe that the relationship would ever change in a way where I would not continue to be hurt. I could not continue to expose myself to repeated emotional pain anymore. I felt confident that I had tried everything I could to try to avoid this outcome.

It was also important to me to continue to check in with Gavin on his reaction to this relationship separation from my parents. I continued to tell Gavin that it was OK for him to be sad, mad, or confused, and to be open with me about it. What continued to amaze me and make me proud was that Gavin was so very understanding and trusting of me. He understood that I had made a hard decision that was ultimately the right one for me, Gavin, and Tom. This separation from my parents opened the door for deeper conversations with Gavin. We talked a lot together about how it was not OK for people to hurt your feelings repeatedly. I coached Gavin on how to handle issues with friends or others who may make him feel bad. I encouraged Gavin to tell the other person how he wanted them to treat him, and if they refused to change how they treated him, it was OK not to play with them anymore or to spend time with other people instead. I wanted Gavin to feel empowered to surround himself with others that lifted him up instead of tearing him down. I also was careful to say that people are allowed to make mistakes and sometimes friends will hurt his feelings. But doing it over and over again and not respecting him was definitely not OK.

As I worked on coping and adjusting to my new reality apart from my parents, I felt like many puzzle pieces started slowly fitting together. Again, being a reflective thinker, I spent countless hours internally processing what had happened and continued to gain insights. As a therapist, I had long pondered what creates an effective working relationship between a therapist and their client. So many of these qualities were the same qualities that create healthy relationships with family and friends. For instance, one of the key tenets I learned in graduate school was that one of the single most defining factors that are linked to effective outcomes in therapy is that the client feels like their therapist "gets it." What this means is that the client believes that their therapist has an authentic understanding of their issues and affirms this to the client.

As I reflected on the relationship with both of my parents and what eventually led to the ending of that relationship, is that my parents did not attempt to "get it." I had long known that my mom did not get me. But what ended up stinging just as much, if not more, was finding out that the very real hope I had had that my dad would be able to understand what I had gone through if I just opened up to him was false. To be let down in such an extreme way by my dad who refused to even try to be open to understanding my own experience almost hurt more. It hurt more because I really believed he had the capability to understand me in a way my mom did not. Finding out that this wasn't the case was crushing to me. When you finally speak your truth and the people who are supposed to care about you only respond with rejection and criticism, it really cuts to the core.

Additional symbolism came from my experience as a therapist as well. Another hallmark tenet of effective and helpful therapy is that the therapist conveys to the client something called "unconditional positive regard." By providing unconditional positive regard to the client, the therapist shows that they recognize the inherent value of the client, accept the client for who they are, and believe the client has the capability for personal growth. This doesn't mean that the therapist thinks the client can do no wrong. Instead, it means that they show that they will accept them and help them despite what faults they possess. Many of these same theories apply to showing unconditional love to your children as a parent. Parents are expected to love and care for their children no matter what. All parents know there are days you may not agree with your child, may be downright angry at them, or even not like them very much. But at the end of the day, your love for your children is something that can't be altered by anything. With the relationship with my mom, I never felt like she had unconditional love or regard for me. I spend a large majority of my life feeling like I was a nuisance to my mom, someone to be endured, not enjoyed. Growing up with a mother that I never felt liked or appreciated me left me feeling inadequate. That there must be something inherently wrong with me. It resulted in a pattern of profound self-doubt over the years. It took me until finally going to therapy after I had become a mother myself to realize how greatly this had all affected me.

Once I had finally connected the dots in terms of how my relationship with my mother had contributed to my lack of self-worth, I could now find ways to repair this. Through my own therapy with Delia, I began to explore what I actually liked about myself. This was not an easy thing to verbalize. I had long learned that flying under the radar and trying to be an average Joe was the best way to protect myself from harsh criticism and further emotional hurt. I was never the most outspoken person in the room and did not love drawing attention to myself. To push myself out of my own comfort zone, I began doing a lot more reading. I completed personality inventories to clarify and validate what made me unique. I talked with Tom and my friends, who I felt really knew my authentic self in a way my mother never did. They helped reflect characteristics that make me the person I am.

I felt through this exercise that I was finally able to confidently say what made me special and unique. Delia helped me realize that one of the big things my mom hadn't provided to me while I was growing up was a reflection of what I was good at or what made me special.

My mom never told me, "Oh you're so creative!" or "You have a great love for reading!" or "You are an excellent sister!"

I never heard feedback about what made me ME. Delia helped me gain awareness that most mothers do this, and it helps foster self-esteem and self-awareness in their children.

I made it my mission to be able to identify what made me who I am today. One of the first things I realized I could confidently say about myself was that I am someone who makes things happen. I am not a procrastinator and thrive on powering through to-do lists. If you need something done, I'm your woman. This is what always helped me finish assignments on time in school. It helped my wedding day go off without a hitch because of being prepared. It's also what helps me keep up with juggling the schedules of the people in my home, especially an active kid.

I am also in my core an assertive communicator. This was something that took more exploration to be able to admit. Many people throughout the years had called me shy. I detested being called shy. To me, shyness was a negative quality. It insinuated that someone was weak, nervous, and had nothing to say. What my husband and friends know about me, though, is something very different from shyness. They know that I hate having tension in relationships or conflicts that are ongoing. Instead, my husband knows all too well that if we have a disagreement, we are going to work it out forthright and not sweep it under the rug. Thankfully I married a man who is a wonderful communicator and I credit both of our strengths in these areas to how strong our marriage is over a decade in now. We do not hold onto grudges and instead use our unique strengths to create compromises to meet both of our needs. I assertively verbalize my needs to others because ultimately, I feel like the more I communicate, the more I open others up to communicating back to me what they need from me. I think on some level, the know-how that I had spent so many of my growing up years holding in my thoughts and feelings for fear of judgment, that now as an adult I intentionally chose to act differently. I didn't want to spend the rest of my life being inauthentic, so acted the opposite as an adult than I had as a child.

Friends know that I wear my heart on my sleeve and if I have a problem with something in our relationship, I am going to say something about it. They never have to wonder if I'm mad at them or unhappy about something going on between us. If I have a frustration, I'm going to put it out in the open because I feel confident that it's easier to take the leap to address it directly than let it stew and fester. I carried around a great deal of inner tension that I knew this about myself but never felt like I could authentically express this characteristic with my parents, especially with my mom. Then when I finally worked up the courage to assertively communicate my feelings to my parents, to be shot down was so defeating.

I do still struggle with my inner voice. That inner voice likes to be timid, hesitant, uncertain, and often, downright critical. When I walked into a hot yoga class for the first time a few years ago at a new gym I joined, I was intimidated. I didn't bring my own yoga mat and couldn't find where they kept the spare ones that I could borrow. There were already tons of women in the studio dressed in nicer, fancier workout gear than me.

I wondered, "Do I look like a sloppy schlep in my old volleyball t-shirt and workout pants with paint stains?"

As the yoga class began, it was clear some of the women were yoga pros, bending themselves into precise pretzels. I was not a newbie to yoga but was certainly not on par with these women. That inner critical voice was strong that day. But one thing I learned as I asserted myself with my mom, was that I didn't have to let that inner voice win. I told that inner voice that I was brave in trying something new. That the first time you do something, there's always going to be some awkwardness. But I did it. I made it through that yoga class and felt outstanding, physically and mentally, afterward. My body had gotten a workout, but my mind had gotten a workout too by conquering the negative inner voice.

As I was now well into my thirties, I slowly felt like I could be proud of what made me special and unique. What I realized was that I had always had big ideas but lacked the courage and confidence to make them happen. I finally felt a fire lit inside me that I could no longer ignore. I knew that I wanted to get more involved in my community. I wanted to give back and help others in a way that could make a positive difference in the world.

I started noticing activism groups more readily and felt a strong tug to get involved. I joined my local chapter of Moms Demand Action for Gun Sense in America as I had long been concerned about the ever-present risk of gun violence. My own son had been practicing intruder and shooter drills since preschool. It sickened me to think that this gun violence problem was continuing without improvement. At my first meeting with Moms Demand Action, I found like-minded people who were also courageous in getting out there and spreading the word and fighting for change. I felt inspired to take things one step further and became a trained speaker giving presentations on Be SMART, a curriculum developed by Moms Demand Action on ways to keep our kids safe regarding guns. I had always had a huge fear of public speaking. But I pushed myself to battle through this fear and remember that what I was working on was more important than what was holding me back. I felt such a great sense of purpose in doing this work and that just reinforced in me that pushing myself beyond my comfort zone really paid off.

Around this time, I was approaching my ten-year anniversary at my job. I had fallen into a corporate job where I was using my therapy license in my role, but not in the way I found meaningful. I was doing case management and felt uninspired and not challenged anymore. I had begun to dread starting work each day and at the end of the day felt depleted. I had noticed a little voice in the back of my head for some time urging me to make a job change. But I had such fear of the unknown. I had a stable income, consistent work hours, and got to work from home which was so valuable in balancing work and family life. I didn't know if I could ever find another job that also provided those same things. To me, the fear of the unknown was greater than the dread of continuing in the job I no longer liked but at least knew what to expect.

I talked to Tom about this conundrum and as always, Tom was completely supportive of whatever I decided was right. I also think that without Tom's encouragement to take a leap of faith, I probably would have just stayed at the steady, consistent job I didn't like, rather than trying for something better. But because he was so encouraging of me, I began to dream bigger. I had had a desire for some time to open my own psychotherapy private practice. I wanted to transition back into more direct care for clients and felt like I had learned a lot in my most recent job that I could use to benefit my clients. I also wanted to be able to be my own boss and set my own work hours. I yearned to be able to have more time to spend with Gavin while he was still young (and let's be frank, while he still wanted to spend time with me!).

An interesting possibility came to me through my research into what it may take to start my own private practice. I learned more about online therapy and how it was growing exponentially as people's reliance and comfort with technology also increased. I had long felt comfortable using technology and realized that if my private practice used an online counseling format, I could continue to work from home. This would give my clients the added flexibility to see me for our sessions from wherever they wanted. It was a win-win situation. I was still worried about losing my current consistent salary and having more of a fluctuating salary in private practice. Tom and I studied our finances closely and realized that we could definitely financially make things work.

From there, I felt a new enthusiasm and burst of energy. I felt inspired to dive headfirst into the planning stages of opening my own practice. My organizational skills and get-things-done attitude became invaluable as I forged ahead with learning what goes into actually opening a small business. After several months of behind-the-scenes business preparation steps, I was finally ready to give my notice at my day job and officially open my practice. I can't fully express the level of freedom and excitement I felt putting my old job behind me. I noticed immediately a weight lifted off my shoulders and a renewed sense of motivation to work hard in my new venture. The reality is that I don't know if I could have or would have ever taken this leap of faith if I hadn't had the courage to address the issues in the relationship with my parents. Instead, I likely would have defaulted to just keeping on keeping on in my unfulfilling job because that was the safe choice. But by proving to myself that I could do hard things and could take risks that would later pay off, I felt more confident to tackle this new job venture.

For the first time in my mere thirty-some years, I felt like my life was one I was happy with. Truly happy. Sure, there were bumps in the road. Everyone has them. But I felt better able to weather those storms knowing that I had made it through a hurricane already with my parents. I knew that whatever curve balls life had in store for me, I would find a way to get through it. I had a support system I trusted. I was living a life with authenticity. I was finally able to be myself in all facets of my life. I no longer had this cloud hanging over my head worrying about everything to do with the dynamics with my mother. There was a freedom and strength I felt in being able to speak my truth. At the end of the day, I could trust my experience and rest in the fact that I had made a decision that was right for me, Tom, and Gavin. Life would keep moving forward. I had the confidence to keep going. I may not have had the mother I wanted or needed, but I was not going to let that hold me back anymore. I was forging my own path, finding healing along the way.

And as Gavin would remind me each time that I picked him up from school, as he excitedly shouted to his friends when he would see me coming, "That's my mom!" took on a whole new meaning.

Acknowledgments

Writing is a labor of love that gives back all the fruits of its labor. I am beyond grateful to the people in my life who have helped me be able to write this book, both in ways seen and unseen.

First and foremost, I never would have written this book had it not been for my encouraging and relentlessly positive husband, Tom. You held my hand as I lived out this memoir both in real-time and as I brought it back to life in print. Your support helped give me the courage to face my struggles and heal from them. Thank you for pushing me forward despite my own doubts along the way. I love you forever.

There are more thanks owed than you will ever know, my dear son, Gavin. You made me a mama. You showed me what unconditional parent-child love looks like. You make me laugh every single day with your voice impressions and Jim Gaffigan's "Hot Pocket" renditions. Your dimpled smile melts my heart. You have given me more gray hair than I ever could have imagined. But I wouldn't trade any of it. You hold a piece of my heart everywhere you go.

To my WOWZAs (Women of Wild Zany Adventures), Becky, Bethany, Rachel, Susan, Kirstyn, Sarah, LeElla, and Anna. You are more than friends. You are the sisters I never had. You are who I go to with good news, bad news, and everything in between. I am beyond grateful for our never-ending Facebook message chat that has been going on for years, and if printed in hard copy, could surely fill a library. Thank you for being my cheerleaders as I shared my dream of writing a book. You were so patient and encouraging reading this book in its early stages and helping me narrow down book cover ideas. I am beyond blessed by each one of you.

An enormous thank you to my editor, Lisa Mullenneaux. Without your help translating my ceaseless babbling into a purposeful coherent story, I would never have made it to this point. Your feedback and perspective were beyond helpful, and I am very grateful.

To the coaches who mentor and lead young people in sports, you are inspiring kids in ways you may not even realize. I was blessed with two of the best, Dave Bauer, and Betsy Emerson. Your positive attitudes, tough love when needed, and never give up mindsets shaped me from a sluggish, quiet cross-country runner barely able to make it to the finish line, to a confident, positive, (slightly) faster runner who wasn't afraid to chase her dreams.

My faith community at Immanuel Lutheran Church has been a source of strength and care for me for almost two decades. Especially as I confronted my concerns with my mother, they were there to lend an ear, share a prayer, and provide hope. I am especially grateful to my pastors and faith group.

A big shout out to my fellow therapists doing the tremendously important and often equally tremendously difficult work of helping clients navigate their mental health. Your work is vital and noble, and I am grateful to all those who mentored me along the way and those who continue to encourage and guide my work today.

Last, but not least, thank you to all the moms out there. Thanks to the biological moms, adoptive moms, stepmoms, sisters, cousins, aunts, grandmothers, neighbors, friends, teachers, coaches, and anyone else living out the role of a mom (that goes for dads too!). My gratitude goes out to moms doing the thankless, tireless, never-ending job of raising humans. Keep on loving them, keep on trying, and the rest will fall into place. You don't have to be perfect. You just have to show up, make mistakes, learn from your mistakes, and keep love at the forefront.

References

Anderman, E. M. (2002). School effects of psychological outcomes during adolescence. *Journal of Educational Psychology, 94,* 795–809.

Aron, E. (1997). The Highly Sensitive Person. Broadway Books.

Ashby, J. S., LoCicero, K. A., & Kenny, M. C. (2003). The Relationship of multidimensional perfectionism to psychological birth order. *The Journal of Individual Psychology, 59* (1), 42-51.

Assor, A., Roth, G., & Deci, E. (2004). The emotional costs of parents' conditional regard: a self-determination theory analysis. *Journal of Personality, 72* (1), 47-88.

Blos, P. (1979). The adolescent passage. New York: *International Universities Press, 26* (3), 227-228.

Brown, B.(2019). Braving the Wilderness. Random House.

Buchanan, C.M., Maccoby, E.E., & Dornbusch, S.M. (1991). Caught between parents: adolescents' experience in divorced homes. *Child Development, 62,* 1008-1029.

Cori, J.(2017). The Emotionally Absent Mother. The Experiment.

Dallos, R., Lakus, K., Cahart, M., McKenzie, R. (2011).Becoming Invisible: The Effect of Triangulation on Children's Well–Being. *Clinical Child Psychology and Psychiatry, 21* (3), 461-476.

Flowers, R. A. & Brown, C. (2002). Effects of sport context and birth order on state anxiety. *Journal of Sport Behavior, 25* (1), 41-56.

Gfroerer, K. P., Gfroerer, C.A., Curlette, W. L., White, J., & Kern, R. M. (2003). Psychological birth order and the BASIS-A Inventory. *The Journal of Individual Psychology, 59* (1), 30-41.

Gladd, I. (2017, November 17). *How to build an emotional connection.* Everyday Health. https://www.everydayhealth.com/emotional-health/how-build-em otional-connection/

Liu, J., Chen, X., & Lewis, G. (2011). Childhood internalizing behaviour: analysis and implications. *Journal of Psychiatric and Mental Health Nursing, 18* (10), 884–894.

Páez D, Velasco C, González JL. (1999). Expressive writing and the role of alexithymia as a dispositional deficit in self-disclosure and psychological health. *Journal of Personality and Social Psychology, 77* (3), 630–641.

Salmon, C. (2003). Birth order and relationships. *Human Nature, 14* (1), 73-88.

Stewart, A. E., Stewart, E. A., & Campbell, L. F. (2001). The relationship of psychological birth order to the family atmosphere and to personality. *The Journal of Individual Psychology, 57* (4), 363-387.

Van der Kolk, B. (2015). The Body Keeps the Score: Brain, Mind, and Body in the Healing of Trauma. Penguin Publishing Group.

Winston, R. & Chicot, R. (2016).The importance of early bonding on the long-term mental health and resilience of children. *London Journal of Primary Care, 8* (1), 12–14.

About the Author

Jacqueline Getchius, M.A., L.P.C.C. is a Licensed Professional Clinical Coun-selor who has worked in the mental health field for eighteen years and is the owner of private practice, Wellspring Women's Counseling, in Minnesota. She provides online counseling to women dealing with perinatal mood disorders, family and parenting concerns, and young adults grappling with life transitions. She has a passion for writing articles spreading mental health education that have been featured on Psych Central. Outside of writing, Jacqueline can be found spending quality time with her favorite guys, her husband, Tom, son, Gavin, and corgi pup, Taco. She loves soaking up the outdoors by running, biking, and doing artsy hobbies like crocheting and painting. You can find more of her writing on her blog: https://wellspringco unseling.online.

Made in the USA
Monee, IL
28 June 2022

98715443R00105